MOTHERS
A CELEBRATION

ALEXANDRA STODDARD

MOTHERS
A CELEBRATION

AVON BOOKS  NEW YORK

AVON BOOKS
A division of
The Hearst Corporation
1350 Avenue of the Americas
New York, New York 10019

Published in hardcover by William Morrow and Company; for information address Permissions Department, William Morrow and Company, Inc., 1350 Avenue of the Americas, New York, New York 10019.

Library of Congress Cataloging in Publication Data:
Stoddard, Alexandra.
   Mothers: a celebration / Alexandra Stoddard
       p.   cm.
1. Mothers.   2. Motherhood.   3. Love, Maternal.   I. Title.
HQ759.S695   1996   95-49856
306.874'3—dc20   CIP

First Avon Books Trade Printing: April 1997

Printed in the U.S.A.

QP 10 9 8 7 6 5 4 3 2 1

To my Zen masters, Alexandra and Brooke,
who continue to teach me how to love,
who fill my heart with happiness
and bring me constant joy.
Being your mother is a precious gift.
I love you. Maman

Contents

Prologue

Mothers, across cultures, are at the
emotional center of the home and,
collectively, of the world. They are
channels of loving energy, the primary
nurturers of all human beings.
Mothers are quintessential people.

One Mother's Experience

Nothing could have adequately prepared me for the love I feel for my two daughters, Alexandra (twenty-nine) and Brooke (twenty-six). They are miracles to me, as all children are. To be their mother is the greatest privilege I will ever know. Nothing can change this powerful feeling nor alter their continuous presence in my soul. Even though my daughters are grown-ups, leading independent lives, the strength we share as a family, as mother and as daughters, is deep, dependable, and eternal.

Being a mother continues to be central to my life. From the moment Alexandra and Brooke were born, I've always felt that I'm in the best company whenever we're together. Now that my time with them is far more limited, I find myself creating new friendships with the children I meet. Their innate goodness, their pure sense of adventure, draw me to them, allowing me to relive many of my favorite aspects of being Alexandra and Brooke's mom.

The Maternal Instinct

At a flea market in Stonington, Connecticut, my husband, Peter, found a brass sculpture of a woman cupping her two children tightly against her body. He said it reminded him of me with Alexandra and Brooke when they were young and I was like a lioness protecting my cubs from the world. I wanted to do everything in my power to make sure their childhood would be as bright and sunny and as full of adventure as possible.

While the literal "hands-on" role of mothering lasts approximately twenty years, the relationship, the bond, and the commitment are forever. Every ounce of love a mother gives to her child nourishes, reinforces, encourages, and teaches not only her child but herself. There are really no boundaries to a mother's loving energy, and in turn, there is nothing more rewarding than a child's adoration. Alexandra and Brooke have lifted me up on their angel wings, raising my spirit, deepening my sense of the mystery, wonder, and grace of life.

My children opened depths in my heart I didn't even know existed. They continue to teach me about the nature of unconditional love. They delight me with their spirit, their goodness, their humor, their smiles, their laughter, and their minds. I'm touched by their tenderness, thoughtfulness, caring natures, and loyalty, all of which grows and multiplies endlessly.

Now that they are adults, I can safely say that to the degree I love life, I learned pure exhilaration from my daughters. The demands of the home are largely behind me and, as hard as it was, and tiring, there's not a day that I don't miss having my "babies in the nest." What I miss most is the laughter, the tears, the ecstasy, the sense of living presence that fills the air in a home where there are children.

I've recently had the joy of having two toddlers excitedly jump into my outstretched arms, smelling of sunshine, kissing and hugging me, playing with my hair, my necklace, and my scarf. This is maternal delight of the purest kind. The sheer pleasure of being in their presence, becoming a part of their world, is all anyone ever needs to know of love and happiness.

The Maternal Bond

I've talked to mothers all over the country, asking questions, trying to clarify the sacred gift that motherhood truly is. As we shared our stories, I became more aware of a far greater, universal love generated by our role as nurturers. When we're able to sense the magnitude of this loving energy, we appreciate our role as mothers, holding a central place in the continuity of life. Nothing compares to being a mother. It is the greatest achievement of my life.

Together, let's celebrate what it is to be a mother. There is no more important work than raising the next generation. This is what mothers do.

The Infinite Influence of Mothers

You know that the beginning is the most part of
any work, especially in the case of a young and tender
thing; for that is the time at which the character is
being formed and the desired impression is more
readily taken. . . .

Anything received into the mind at that age is
likely to become indelible and unalterable...models
of virtuous thoughts. . . .

Then will our youth dwell in a land of health,
amid fair sights and sounds, and receive the good
in everything; and beauty, the effluence of fair works,
shall flow into the eye and ear, like a health-giving
breeze from a purer region, and insensibly draw
the soul from the earliest years into likeness and
sympathy with the beauty of reason.

—Plato's Republic

Mothers

Chapter 1

Honoring and Loving Our Mothers

Whereas the service rendered the United States by the American mother is the greatest source of the country's strength and admiration; and Whereas we honor ourselves and the mothers of America when we do anything to give emphasis to the home; and Whereas the American mother is doing so much for good government and humanity, we declare that the second Sunday of May will henceforth be celebrated as Mother's Day.

—Presidential Proclamation, 1914

I dedicated my book *Living a Beautiful Life* to my mother, Barbara Green Johns, because she had, among other things, a great sense of style. Her love of beauty, her pleasure in the quality of the light and in the design of all things, combined with her practical sense of homemaking, added immeasurably to our family's daily life. Mother was not only handy but wonderfully creative. Growing up on our rambling onion farm, I felt all my senses were stimulated by my mother's love of gardening, cooking, art, and antiques. In the evening, Mother loved to sit in the living room by the fire doing embroidery, needlepoint, or petit point; but just as often she would be darning a sock or sewing a button. A family of six required maintenance. Mother lived by the theory "A stitch in time saves nine." She tightened our loose buttons before they popped off and reinforced our hems before they tore.

Mother is the name for God in the lips and hearts of children.

—William Makepeace Thackeray

I loved to keep her company when I was eight, nine, and ten, working on my own extremely intricate sampler which she designed especially for me. I still have the yarn basket I used. Our home was always infused with an air of warmth and charm.

My mother was a strong, beautiful, smart, and powerful woman. Few people were more organized or had a greater capacity for enthusism. She was gutsy, inquisitive, and persevering. Her intellectual curiosity made everything in our home more meaningful, more rich, more lively and exciting. Though my mother was only an adequate cook—I learned basic cooking skills from her—she preferred to do other things with her time. Instead of having a cookbook as a bible, my mother always kept an open dictionary on the counter. Mother was more interested in cooking words than food. We'd play word games. Though I don't think Mother's heart was ever in the kitchen, she made it so by having and using that dictionary.

Mother also loved cars, primarily for the freedom they represented to her. Her favorite car was a 50s silver Jaguar with red leather interiors. She was fascinated by that car. I have vivid memories of her washing it in the driveway, chamois rag in hand. The reverence she had for that beautiful car verged on obsession. She polished the leather seats, a gleam of pleasure in her eyes. She even enjoyed waxing the carpathian elm burl wood of the dashboard. What a treat to be invited on a toot just after she'd washed the car. She'd take me on several of her favorite scenic roads, beaming with joy and pride. On these adventures, my mother would lose all sense of time. Behind the wheel of her car, Mother basked in glory.

Happy he/With such a mother. Faith in womankind/ Beats with his blood, and trust in all things high/Comes easy to him.

— Alfred, Lord Tennyson

As it turned out, most of my mother's talents and interests became my own (except for the cars). There is no question that her passion for beauty, fine art, the decorative arts, and her innate sense of style rubbed off on me. With her near me every day, tutoring me in the decorative arts, it was natural for me to go on to study interior design. She also loved gardening with a passion. I watched her pore over seed catalogs and packages. When I was three years old watching my mother's flower garden grow, I knew I wanted to have one, too. Because she made a deliberate effort to guide and direct my path, I was exposed to a wealth of knowledge and inspiration around the subtle nuances of taste and beauty.

In virtue alone is happiness... never was an existence upon earth more blessed than my mother's.

— John Quincy Adams

Mother was never one to quit. I've never known anyone as hardworking, tough-minded, and determined. She believed you get energy by expending energy. I consider myself strong and well grounded thanks to the canvas painted by my mother for herself and for those she loved. She was a living portrait of character, integrity, and grace. Despite her firmness, I always went to bed knowing I was loved.

The Blessings Mothers Bestow

Whenever Peter wants to tell anyone anything of importance, Miriam, his mother, is woven into the story. Peter was also blessed with a wonderful mother. Of all the many gifts she gave him, her happiness and her unconditional love were at the top of the list. Miriam loved being a mother. She was in her ele-

Mother was one of those strong, restful, yet widely sympathetic natures, in whom all around seemed to find comfort and repose.

— Harriet Beecher Stowe

ment whenever she and her children were together. Her love of them was an obvious pleasure. She was an undemanding, uncontrolling, and noncritical presence in their close, tight relationships. The atmosphere was perfumed with mutual delight. What greater boost to a child than to be loved and adored by his mother? And how wonderful to know that you, as her child, have contributed so much to her happiness.

Miriam had a gift for happiness. She found life a delight and that delight spread to her children. She painted landscapes and portraits in oil, she hand-painted furniture and decorative objects, and she did needlework and petit point, as did my mother. She designed her own jewelry while also raising her children. She always enjoyed the varied rituals of home — planning holiday celebrations, family trips, and parties for friends. Being a mother was Number One to her, the top priority of her life. She loved nurturing her four children, accepting the heartaches as well as relishing the sweet times. She wasn't concerned with "having it all." She had what she wanted and she knew it. When Miriam was in her eighties, she told Peter that the happiest time in her life was spent sitting at the round kitchen table in their small house in Shaker Heights, Ohio, with all her children underfoot.

Miriam's children were all born in the 1920s, a time when husbands supported the family and the wife was expected to stay at home. Miriam's life had clear structure, boundaries, and harmony. But somehow I think Miriam's gifts as a mother had more to do with her than with her times.

Miriam may have lived in a different era, but we can still learn a lot from a woman who not merely accepted the cards life dealt her, but who made the most of her hand. Even when her son George was a prisoner of war in Japan for two years and she presumed he was dead, she tried to prevent the children from seeing her anguish, fostering an atmosphere of hope and honor in his absence. She focused on what she had right in front of her, within reach, concentrating on her charity and church work. Peter received countless letters from her when he was in the army, all newsy and lovable. She always had the support of family and friends—her daughters had recently married naval officers—and throughout it all, she remained the glue that held everybody together.

Because Miriam and Peter always got along and enjoyed each other's company, they saw a great deal of each other. Before I saw it for myself, I couldn't believe how much fun they had together. Eventually, I discovered their secret, although it took me a while. Miriam was crazy about Peter, and he about her. This mutual affection, this appreciation for each other's worth, put a twinkle in their eyes whenever they were together.

Peter's love for his mother and the depth of their relationship was so important to him that he decided to dedicate a memoir to her and write about her in one of the essays it contained. After agonizing at first about how to begin a topic so emotionally charged, Peter eventually gained some measure of distance. Rather

All mothers are quintessential: In pain and joy they are always with us, encouraging, instructing, loving.

— Peter Megargee Brown

than using *mother*, he chose to call her Miriam throughout his essay, and the words came pouring out of him. He wrote the entire piece in one sitting at his desk in Stonington Village. Memories flowed out of his heart onto his yellow legal pad in a seamless stream of consciousness. Memories of running on the beach with his mother, of watching a street vendor grind horseradish under the Third Avenue El. Those hours that Peter spent writing about Miriam were some of the happiest of his life because he was finally able to capture just how much his mother had given to him, how much she meant to who he was.

> *Beautiful as seemed mamma's face, it became incomparably more lovely when she smiled, and seemed to enliven everything about her.*
>
> — *Leo Tolstoy*

At Miriam's funeral service at the Church of the Redeemer in Bryn Mawr, Pennsylvania, Peter read some of his favorite passages from this memoir, *Flights of Memory, Days Before Yesterday:*

If you had to characterize Miriam, mostly a dangerous practice, you'd have to say Miriam was an artist most of her life — in the true sense of the word. An artist, who, seemingly without effort, could find color, texture, and balance in proportions that live in the memory long after the time of her creation.

When I last remember talking to Miriam when she was in her nineties, in a garden seat at Dunwoody, a country nursing home near Bryn Mawr, Pennsylvania, I asked her about Father. What were her thoughts after all these years and the end drawing near? She lifted her head and looked out at the oaks and the elms, across the hill. "Whenever you think of someone, he is never dead. That's what memory can do for us."

Afterward, the minister said that he'd never experienced a more detailed or poignant eulogy. There, in that sacred place, was her loving family. Three generations of people's lives had been personally touched by this wonderful woman and mother. Each of us cried as we brought to the surface all our happy times with Grandmother Brown.

My friend John Bowen Coburn, former Episcopal Bishop of Massachusetts, who married Peter and me in 1974 in New York City, wrote me recently of this approach to life which I identify so much as Miriam's: "So...life with its tragedies and glories goes on. Losses we offer up and gains we cherish all the more."

All-gracious! grant to those who bear/A mother's charge, the strength and light/To guide the feet that own their care/In ways of Love and Truth and Right.

— William Cullen Bryant

The Examples Mothers Set

Some of us had good relationships with our mothers, others were strained. The relationship between a mother and son is quite different from the relationship between mother and daughter. Our mothers, for all their love and concern, often lost perspective on us, their daughters. It's natural for mothers to see themselves in their daughters, and sometimes this causes them to transfer their expectations of themselves onto us.

Sometimes when a mother and daughter grow close, the

mother may unwittingly see her daughter as a clone of herself. My mother had this tendency, especially with me because I was the one of her four children most like her.

I recall one day over thirty years ago, early in my career, a local newspaper sent a photographer to our house to take pictures, including a picture of my mother with her two daughters. Proudly, she told the reporter that I was an interior designer in New York, but that someday I might return to Connecticut to work with her. Although I was touched that she had this wishful thought, I knew at the time that I would probably never work with her. The year the photos were published I was doing a lot of design in Washington and I loved the firm where I worked. Several years after Mother's death, I expanded my boundaries and became an international designer.

There is in every true woman's heart, a spark of heavenly fire.

—Washington Irving

When mother and daughter are alike as we were there's a charge of competitiveness in the air. This made me somewhat afraid to be completely myself in front of my mother. I was particularly sensitive to this because my career took off almost immediately, while my mother's didn't have the same jump start. I was at the right place at the right time and I was only twenty-two years old. My mother was married, had raised four children, and even though she was strong-willed, my father, like many men of his genera-

In the man whose childhood has known caresses, there is always a fiber of memory that can be touched to gentle issues.

— George Eliot

tion, didn't want my mother to have a career. So she didn't become established until she was middle-aged, which limited her horizons.

Before my mother died, I came to realize, with her help, that she really didn't have mixed feelings about my career. Mother showed a great deal of interest in my work, and we often talked about design when we were together. When she took a tour of the interiors on the fifty-eighth floor of the Citicorp building, she was moved by the colors, the textures, and the lighting I had designed. I saw that she took pride in my accomplishments. On her coffee table, she kept a stack of magazines containing all the articles about my design work. She wasn't modest about showing her friends examples of some of my jobs. I had, gradually and naturally, moved away from her powerful influence on me, toward myself and my own self-expression. She saw my strength more as an honor to her, a credit to her role as my mother. And indeed, in some way—by no means a straight and easy path—she had helped me to do so, to find my way by her own example.

The greatest difference which I find between my mother and the rest of the people whom I have known is this, and it is a remarkable one: while others felt a strong interest in a few things, she felt a strong interest in the whole world and everything and everybody in it.

— Mark Twain

When the Blessings Are Mixed

I loved my mother dearly, but I am also the first to admit that our relationship, like many mother-daughter relationships, had complexities. My mother had some tough breaks in her life, starting with her father dying of tuberculosis when she was five. She overcame this profound loss in the best way she knew. She became strong and self-reliant because of the hardship of having only one parent. My mother also suffered from a heart murmur and had to leave college because the doctors feared it was too risky for her to be away from the calm, controlled environment of home. Because she was hiding so much of her own pain from her children, she wasn't always emotionally available to us. I was conscious of her struggles and therefore I tried to please her.

Man's love is of man's life a thing apart: 'tis woman's whole existence.

— Lord Byron

Mother worried all the time. Raising four children in a disintegrating marriage is enough to make anyone nervous, frustrated, and angry. But she always tried to focus her fierce energies on keeping the family together, providing us with all the necessary life skills she thought we needed to survive. No one was more organized or capable than Mother, but perhaps she was this way to a fault. Her insistence on keeping our rooms clean bordered on the obsessive. There was a *right* way to set the table, arrange flowers, write thank you notes, dress, behave in front of guests— and there was no arguing with her.

No man is poor who has had a godly mother.

— Abraham Lincoln

I wasn't encouraged to make my own mistakes. If I washed lettuce and threw too many leaves away, she'd prove to me in graphic detail how wasteful I was. She'd clean and dry the lettuce I had discarded and almost fill a salad bowl with my stupidity. When my father was vice president of Elizabeth Arden, we had Blue Grass products spewing out of the linen closet and all medicine cabinets. Even though there was a never-ending supply, I was severely reprimanded for whizzing through an entire can of hair spray. My hair was my addiction. I wore my hair in a ponytail when I played tennis but off the court my blond hair was perfectly groomed, bobbing under in a pageboy, Grace Kelly style. I set my hair in curlers—only when I was upstairs in privacy—and after brushing it out, I'd spray my hair firm, as though it were wired in place. When you're growing up, you do some careless things, but when I look back, I was never really a mess. Actually, I was quite a self-aware person, doing the best I could. But as long as I was sighted, wherever her gyroscope spun, I was vulnerable to criticism. If there were a thousand good things about me, Mother could find some fault and didn't hesitate to make a critical comment.

My mother made a brilliant impression upon my childhood life. She shone for me like the evening star—I loved her dearly....

— Winston Churchill

She wanted us to know right from wrong and good from evil. She wanted us to be strong physically, mentally, and spiritually, to have high moral values, firm character, and be conscientious. We were to be principled, thorough, and careful. Mother's dramatic personality led her to theatrically recite Shakespeare, the Bible, and favorite poems. We were not allowed to be "loose, lazy lumps lying languidly on the lawn, lollygagging in the lap of luxury, licking lollipops." "By gum," we were to shape up!

Mother's word was law and we were definitely discouraged from talking back to her or voicing disagreement. She was very artistically gifted and knew what she wanted, and I found it hard even to attempt to deviate from her standard. I forgive her because she didn't mean any harm.

By the time my mother died I was, at thirty-eight, quite capable of carrying on. And finally, as she lay dying in the hos-

As for the mother, her very name stands for loving unselfishness and self-abnegation and in any scoiety fit to exist, it is fraught with associations which render it holy.

— Theodore Roosevelt

pital, she utterly succumbed to letting her dukes down, yielding to me as a daughter she greatly prized and admired. Her poignant words to me are woven firmly in my heart. I always knew how enormously she loved me, but as my coach and trainer, she tended to push too hard in all directions all the time. She was courageous, plucky, dominating, powerful, and extraordinary, but she was stressed and strained, feeling pressured all the time because of the unrelenting emphasis she placed on everything.

I often wonder what my relationship with my mother would have been like if I'd traveled around the world with *her* instead of my aunt when I was sixteen. Whenever Mother and I did anything together, it strengthened our bond. I bet she would have loved kicking up her heels, leaving home, abandoning her domestic responsibilities to the excitement of foreign lands.

I returned home from my worldly travels at age seventeen, a changed person, a changed daughter. And I'm sure she felt this. It was more than a dozen years before she would travel to Asia and experience the tea ceremony and begin to understand the calming balm of inner peace and Zen.

Many of us have had disagreements with our mothers about everything, including the clothes we wore and how we wore them, how we did in school, the friends we chose, the spiritual paths we followed, how we spent our time and our money. Mother and I held many opposing opinions about many issues, from religion and dating to school. She was also dubious about both my husbands. Rather than rebelling, which would have been self-defeating, I continued to try to behave in such a way as to avoid being punished. I found it was better for me to hide my emotions from her than to risk criticism. Because I was on a spiritual quest of my own from the time I was sixteen and didn't follow her strict religious beliefs, she was apprehensive. She was fearful about my future; always thinking the worst. She worried about everyone I dated, thinking they would each take advantage of me. She insisted that everything be on the "up and up," and no "hanky panky." Even though she was my greatest cheerleader and supporter, it wasn't easy for her to let me go to design school rather than to a liberal arts college. Following my world trip, I completed my studies at the New York School of Interior Design and after graduation got married, never having gone to college. What she didn't realize was that her example of self-education was so exemplary, I knew how to learn on my own, as she did.

I felt outmatched by her, unable to defend myself and win. When I was thirty-two years old, I couldn't confide in her how deeply I loved Peter. We had a huge disagreement on Peter's and my wedding day, when she threatened me and I refused to give in.

Wedding days are usually unnerving. Little things become explosive in such turbulent emotional situations. That day, my mother sent me

A sufficient measure of civilization is in the influence of good women.

— Emerson

The word "Mother" conjures up cozy visions of homespun family life: Mother baking cookies, mother sympathetically listening to your tragedies, mother as your champion.

— Victoria Secunda

off the charts. Devoted to her granddaughters, Alexandra and Brooke, she convinced them that I was absurd to insist they wear their spun-silk hair down with crowns of lily of the valley. There in their bedroom, she put their hair in ponytails, against my wishes. The issue was no longer about the girls' hair. That day I woke up to the realization that she was a *guest* in our apartment and had no right to undermine me, just as I had had to toe the line when I was growing up under her roof.

> *For me, a line from mother is more efficacious than all the homilies preached in Lent.*
>
> *— Henry Wadsworth Longfellow*

Peter and I flew to Paris that evening for the honeymoon. When I woke up the next morning, a newlywed, I vowed to myself she would never have any destructive power over our marriage. We were united, and we were free to live according to our own set of rules. I didn't need her blessing, because every pore of my being informed me what was right for Peter and me.

Later, I came to understand that some of her concerns, which were inconsequential to me, could be normal for a mother. She worried that Peter, who had a very active practice as a trial lawyer, wouldn't have enough time for me. But when he carried my tote bag around the country on the book tour when my first book was published, she saw how devoted he was to me and my interests. I understand now that she acted out of fear for me, though it hurt me nevertheless.

I am struck by how differently my daughters feel from the way I did as a daughter about revealing mistakes and causing my mother disappointment. Several years ago, Alexandra was joking around and said, "Mom, I know you'll still love me even if I get fired from my job." Her words reminded me of the time when I had to tell my mother that I had been fired from my first job as a decorator. I was terrified by the idea of confessing this news to her, causing her worry and doubt. I simply did not want her to feel let down. I did not want her to think that I hadn't made the most of the opportunities she had made available to me in life.

Many of us spend our lives trying to make our mothers proud of us when they really already are. We try to be "easy to love." I lived this way throughout my life. Much later, I learned that we do not honor our mothers by trying to please them, but rather by blossoming within ourselves. Then they can see who we really are and the good work they have done to support us.

No doubt too many of us gave our mothers—and our fathers—good reason to worry sometimes. Some of us lied about where we were spending the evening; we didn't come home on time; we forgot to call; we were sometimes rude and thoughtless. We had wild parties when parents were away, and sometimes the police were called. We'd get into car accidents. I drove the car into a wall in a rainstorm one night because of a hole in the road—and because I was taking a corner too fast on a slippery road. At times, some of us had no choice but to lie to our mother. When I had a date who passed out in the passenger seat because he drank too much, I drove him home. If I had told my mother, would I ever have been allowed to see that young man again? As my daughters say, "I

....everything I did you encouraged. I cannot remember once in my life when you were not interested in what I was working on, or ever suggested that I should put it aside for something else.

– Edna St. Vincent Millay

don't *theenk* so!" We'll never know all the sacrifices, all the sleepless nights, the disappointments and despair we put our mothers through. We shouldn't cast the first stone.

At the same time, mothers were once children and teenagers, too. Mothers may pretend that they were never young and foolish, but they remember through firsthand experience more than their children give them credit for. Mothers have been there. They poignantly remember hundreds of times they frightened *their* parents nearly to death. Sometimes mothers do assume the worst, visualizing all sorts of dangerous situations their children might get themselves into, temporarily forgetting that those children, too, want to avoid being raped, mugged, or otherwise abused. Children have confided in me that far too many adults, including parents and educators, point their fingers at them, assuming they're sexually irresponsible or experimenting with drugs. Children deserve to be trusted until they do something that totally breaches that trust. Then you have to work together to find a way that they can earn back that trust.

I guess what I'm saying is the ball is never entirely in one court. Just as we're never all happy or all sad, the mothers of the world aren't all good or all bad. We're who we are, for better or for worse. But I've never met a normal woman who deliberately tried to ruin her child's life. As awkward as we may be some-

A kiss from my mother made me a painter.

— Benjamin West

The woman who creates and sustains a home, and under whose hands children grow up to be strong and pure men and women, is a creator second only to God.

— Helen Hunt Jackson

times in expressing our love, I'm in favor of forgiveness, of giving mothers the benefit of the doubt. But remember, forgiveness runs both ways. We must understand that a mother is on call for her children twenty-four hours a day, seven days a week. Mothers can't run off and be naughty; there's tremendous pressure on them—as we've come to know as mothers ourselves.

The Gift of Forgiveness

I wasn't always so forgiving of my mother's controlling ways. I finally found a bridge over these troubled waters when my mother took on a new role in my life shortly before she died.

Often, at some important turning point of our lives, we get an opportunity to carve a new path, establish a new link to our mothers. It is a wholly new connection, forged no longer out of our childhood dependence but of our adult respect for our mothers' humanity. Sometimes when we are confronted with our mothers' vulnerability and frailty, either through illness or through some setback, we can see them in new ways. During these crises our traditional roles often change, and we realize that mother no longer has the overwhelming power over us that she had when we were children. We can feel a new freedom—and with that freedom comes compassion. Now it is our turn to care for her. Caring for our mothers, listening to them, and expressing our feelings to them without blame or bitterness frees us of

My mother had a slender, small body, but a large heart—a heart so large that everybody's joys found welcome in it, and hospitable accommodation.

— Mark Twain

the hold of past resentments. We realize we no longer need to play the role we played as children. We can recognize how we, too, have changed over the years and that we have the maturity to allow our parents their strengths as well as their flaws.

When we're able to make this passage, we learn how to be better mothers ourselves. We can learn from our mother's shortcomings—but only when we accept them as they are.

All this I learned when my mother was dying. During this time, Mother continually reminded me of how much she really loved me. She confessed that in many ways, I was living the life she'd envisioned for herself. I had a wonderful marriage partnership, healthy children, and a successful career. While my parents' marriage started out storybook perfect—they were a dynamic, intelligent couple, with four healthy children, who lived in old houses they enjoyed restoring together—over the years things deteriorated. My father wasn't faithful to my mother, which broke her heart, and her youngest child, Richard, was diagnosed with a severe mental illness from which he never recovered. Our conversations made it clear to me how connected we were and how, in a sense, I had continued in her ideal path. She showed me that she trusted me and was confidently able to pass on the baton, believing I wouldn't drop it—but that if I did, I wouldn't do it intentionally. These woman-to-woman conversations were intensely beautiful and I felt fortunate to be there when she opened her heart. She looked toward me as a sign of hope for the future.

> *My mother was the most beautiful woman I ever saw....All I am I owe to my mother.... I attribute all my success in life to the moral, intellectual, and physical education I received from her.*
>
> *— George Washington*

I grew during those weeks when we spoke so openly. I was grateful to learn for the first time that my mother had a taste for adventure, not unlike my own. One rainy April day, she confessed that she had been a wild teenager. "I loved going on motorcycles, smoking, drinking, and having boyfriends," she told me, laughing. "And not always the kind of boys you'd want to take home for Sunday dinner." The only thing that kept her from being really naughty, she told me, was her respect for her mother. "I never wanted to let my mother down." I'm so glad we were able to reach each other; I'm glad to have learned of her exuberant, lively, youthful ways. These stories balance my memory of her as a strict, strong, no-nonsense woman.

I feel that, in the Heavens above, the angels, whispering to one another, can find, among their burning terms of love, none so devotional as that of "Mother."

— Edgar Allan Poe

I, too, was able to share some intimacies. I told my mother about some of my romances, my heartache when, at the age of fifteen, I was ignored by the boy I'd dreamed of marrying. Mother grew to understand that although she'd disciplined me all my life, our relationship had changed; she now intuitively wanted us to share a bond as two women. All her mothering, her "tuck in your blouse" or "stand up straight" or "speak more clearly" was behind us. Now, finally, blessedly, we were equals, enjoying all our connections and differences, appreciating each other's mutual talents, interests, and stories. This soft, warm side of my mother was shining forth as she dropped her role as parent and loved me as an individual person.

A Mother's arms are made of tenderness and children sleep soundly in them.

— Victor Hugo

I was thirty-eight years old when my mother lay in a hospi-

> It was a memory that met us everywhere, for every person in town, from the highest to the lowest, seemed to have been so impressed by my mother's character and life that they constantly reflected some portion of it back on us.
>
> — Harriet Beecher Stowe

tal bed dying. With tears welling up in her eyes she said, "Oh, Sandie dear, I haven't taught you everything yet." So, right to the end, Barbara Green Johns was still my mother. Those private talks sitting on the bed in the hospital, one-on-one with Mother, were some of the most meaningful mother-daughter times we ever had together. While she was still my mother, the realization of her imminent death, her fragility, helped her to become more human to me. She let her guard down and opened herself up.

This changing of roles was a timely gift to my mother and me. From her hospital bed she expressed her appreciation for all the fruits of her labors. I sensed her expanded faith and confidence in me. Mother died really knowing her younger daughter better. I felt I had lost a good friend. What a blessing it was to forgive.

It wasn't until after my mother died that I fully made peace with our differences and could fully appreciate her positive, integral influence on me.

I also learned—and have kept this in my mind as a mother—that our children help us to become thoughtful about what's real.

Our Mothers as Real People

Our bond with our mothers begins in the first moments of our lives. Our mothers are a blessed necessity. We draw our primary strength from our mothers' love. Their love literally keeps us alive when we are infants. Throughout history, genius and greatness literally have been nurtured by the hands that rocked the cradle. Our mothers do indeed play a major part in our success and happiness.

In some ways, we never outgrow the need for mother love. We just have to find it in different places. There are times when Peter wants to be mothered, wanting bouillon brought to him in bed when he's not feeling well. I love it when the girls pamper me in instinctively maternal ways, rubbing my feet with cream, telling me everything's going to be all right. We all benefit throughout our lives from the continuity of mother love.

My mother was as mild as any saint, and nearly canonized by all she knew, So gracious was her tact and tenderness.

— Alfred, Lord Tennyson

When a mother can unabashedly love and express that affection to her child, joy results. But mothers are human, too. They make mistakes. They have problems they cannot overcome. They worry too much. They can't always help doing what they do. They care too much, which, in a strange way, is why they have such awesome influence in their children's lives. Mothers by definition love, care, console, teach, nurture, provide, protect, and put others first.

While we are aware of the dark side of our mothers, I think it's important to dwell instead on their virtues. No matter how many mistakes they've made or how unfairly we think we were treated, if we look closely, we can see that while the mother-daughter bond isn't always the eas-

His sweetest dreams were still of that dear voice that soothed his infancy.

— Robert Southey

2 5

Grace was in all
her steps,/Heaven
in her eye,/
In every gesture
dignity and love.

— John Milton

iest, it is filled with power and potential. Mothers deserve our honor and respect.

We who become mothers can learn from our experiences with our own parents. As mothers ourselves, we learn that the best we can do is to *do* our best and hope that despite what we may fail to do, our children will feel it's always possible to talk with us, to reach a loving place.

There isn't a day that goes by when I don't think of my mother, when I don't miss her gumption, her verve, her energy, and enthusiasm. "Darling Sandie, I've never done anything in my life in half measures," she said when she was told she'd die within a few months. She continues to guide me, inspire me, and love me. I honor and respect this strong woman; I hold her in great esteem. I recognize her dignity, her honor, and her great capacity to avoid openly feeling sorry for herself, no matter how hurt she was inside. I recognize her distinction, her excellence, and eminence. A defining factor in my life is what a difference this one woman made in helping me along my path.

A mother is an
epiphany.

— Peter
Megargee Brown

As I salute *my* mother, I celebrate and honor *all* mothers. After all, from the beginning, now and forever, mothers do the most honorable work on earth. In raising children, they tap into heavenly virtues, playing the key part in creation.

Chapter 2

How Motherhood Transforms Us

Truth, which is important to a scholar, has got to be concrete. And there is nothing more concrete than dealing with babies, burps and bottles, frogs and mud.

—Jeane J. Kirkpatrick

Expanding Our Commitment to Life

Becoming a mother is absolutely the most demanding experience you can have in life, but it is also one of the most exhilarating and profound. When my newborn first child, Alexandra, was placed in my arms, I felt a depth of boundless love and protectiveness for her that I had never known before. She seemed a miracle to me, this tiny new life that was all mine to care for. Like a new lover, I celebrated every inch of her: every facial expression, her radiant eyes, her tiny fingers, her movements, and her smile. Oh, that baby smile!

An outward and visible sign of an inward and spiritual grace.

— The Book of Common Prayer

I dreamed of all the wonderful things in the world I would introduce to her: sharing with her the pleasure of her first bite of chocolate cake; watching her thrill at her first sight of the ocean and her first leap into the waves; witnessing her joy upon learning to say her first words and reading her first books.

*Being a mother,
as far as I
can tell, is a
constantly
evolving process
of adapting to the
needs of your
child while also
changing and
growing as a
person in your
own right.*

— Deborah Insel

I wanted my newborn baby to have everything. In that spirit, I had painted her nursery sunshine yellow, filled it with white wicker furniture, and installed two indoor window boxes filled with trailing ivy geraniums. I was overjoyed strolling with her in the bright-blue baby carriage a friend had loaned me, around which I had carefully draped a hot-pink-and-yellow bunting. It was my first expression of wanting her to appreciate what was good in life—all its light and beauty.

I wanted everything for my child. In turn, she would ask everything of me. "Our chief want in life," observed Ralph Waldo Emerson, "is somebody who shall make us do what we can." The weight of my commitment to Alexandra, and later to Brooke, awakened my commitment to be my best in everything. It asked that I go the extra mile to be more responsible, more reliable, more reasonable, more patient, honest, and devoted than I ever believed possible.

We are called upon by our children, time and again, to bring all our gifts and strengths in support of their growing life. Children require our all. Being a mother humbles us with its great demands, but it also helps us to enlarge our capabilities. For our children we must tap into our higher selves and find abilities we never knew we had. A mother must rise above herself. Sometimes, she must wipe away a child's tears, just when she wants someone to do the same for her.

Your child has the potential to make you feel capable, generous, to give of yourself unconditionally. Even though you may feel pushed to your limits, somehow, as a mother, you find it within yourself to regenerate emotional and physical energy for your child. Doing so, in a sense constitutes a renewal of your commitment to life. But your child helps you to do this as well. By their love, their need, and expectations of us, and by their own acts of courage in taking new steps, our children inspire us to do more than we otherwise might.

Life, at best, becomes a divine balancing act in order to create wisdom and harmony.

Becoming a mother changes everything about your life. Motherhood deepens your connection to all of life, making you a more active participant in both the joys and pains of living. You seek out things in the world that will enhance your child's life and pleasure, becoming a frequent visitor to parks and museums, a reader of books on whales and dinosaurs, an avid eater of ice cream and a singer of songs, a hiker, and a tree climber. You also see the insides of doctors' offices and even hospitals more often than you'd like, stay up later and wake up earlier than you ever cared to, and sustain patience even as chaos constantly threatens to erupt around you. It is not always easy, but you can find no greater sense of being fully alive than in what is asked of you in being a mother.

Once you are a mother, you also feel a greater vulnerability to all of life. You worry about everything from the weather to the cars on the street. You also wonder about your own vulnerabilities: Will I be a good enough mother? Will I have the courage to face the challenges? Will I have the patience to work things

When a child enters the world through you, it alters everything on a psychic, psychological and purely practical level.

— Jane Fonda

through? What if my child gets sick? How will I be able to leave her with a baby-sitter? How will I be able to understand her when she is an adolescent? What if the schools in my community are not good enough? What if I do not like her friends? The list goes on.

You will wear many hats— including that of lifelong learner.

— Greta K. Nagel

When Alexandra was four, she became dangerously sick with pneumonia and had a raging fever. All my strength and resolve was turned toward her. I paced up and down the hall of the hospital as my child lay in an oxygen tent. I was completely there for her and somehow I knew that by being so, I could help her heal. As mothers, whether we must face a minor or major problem of any kind, we know that there isn't anything we wouldn't do for our children, and this gives us the strength and courage we need.

"The babe in arms is a channel through which the energies we call fate, love, and reason, visibly stream," observed Emerson. Becoming a mother opens those channels. I grew light years during Alexandra and Brooke's childhoods.

Being Interrupted

When we choose to become mothers we are choosing to be interrupted, to give love when love is needed, to listen when listening is demanded, to drop what we're doing when children need our attention. And sometimes we realize that we have to take a backseat to our children's growth. Our time is no longer our own, at least not like it used to be: We cannot run out and take an aerobics class or go to the museum or meet a friend for a drink, just anytime. For some of us, this constitutes a real sacrifice; loving our children doesn't mean we won't miss the pleasures we enjoyed before. But we understand that we have given up some of this freedom by our own choice, and that choice pleases us deeply.

> *I love being a mother... I am more aware. I feel things on a deeper level. I have a kind of understanding about my body, about being a woman.*
>
> *— Shelley Long*

My friend Marysarah frequently used to hop on a train from Penn Station in New York to visit us in our cottage in Stonington, Connecticut. We always had a great time during her visits. Last year when she became a new mother, I reminded her that she's always welcome to visit us. She replied, "I know. You are so sweet to ask. But now that I have Dylan, everything's different. I just want to go home to see him, even though I still adore being with you."

Nineteenth-century philosopher William James explained the phenomenon of a mother's instinct to sacrifice when he observed:

> Make a mother of her, and what have you? Possessed by maternal excitement, she now confronts wakefulness, weariness, and toil without an instant of hesitation or a word of complaint. The inhibitive power of pain over her is extinguished whenever the baby's interests are at stake.

A mother is on constant duty to monitor the continual shifts in her child's needs: from hunger to satisfaction, tears to smiles, boredom to activity. She serves her young child's schedule, not her own. When it comes to being a mother, we are the workers, not the boss!

When Alexandra screamed until her face turned beet red, I'd rush to check her diaper, sure a safety pin had popped open and was sticking her to death. If that wasn't the problem, I'd try to see if she was hungry, had soiled diapers, had colic, you name it. I would have jumped through hoops if it would have made her stop crying. Our doctor told us she was just developing her lungs. So, when she cried, after checking to make sure she wasn't ill, wet, or hungry, I'd turn on the radio, do the dishes, and generally create enough noise around me to drown out the shrieks. Sometimes, she simply needed to cry herself out and go to sleep. Not every doctor tells you to do the same thing. By trial and error you figure out how to tame the savage moods of your little one.

When a child enters your life, everything gets complicated. When it's raining, everyone must have rain slickers and umbrellas. Just leaving the house to go to school requires that we run down a checklist of needs: Does everyone have their lunch? A jacket in case it gets cold? One child has a play date requiring another set of clothes, while the other child wants to be home with you to bake a cake (and did you buy the cake mix?) A day at the beach becomes a packing nightmare—never mind a trip to the country. There's always something forgotten, something that hasn't been considered. It happens even at home. I remember one evening, when Alexandra was three weeks old, as we were say-

> *...that wild, unknown being, the child.*
>
> — *Colette*

> *Only a mother knows a mother's fondness.*
>
> — *Lady Mary Wortley Montagu*

ing good night to friends after dinner, we walked them to the elevator and the apartment door slammed shut, locking our helpless infant inside and us out in the hall. It was winter. I had on velvet slippers, had no money, no coat, and no discernable access to a locksmith. We were scared to death. When there's a child around, every move we make has consequences.

There's a lot more to being a woman than being a mother, but there's... a lot more to being a mother than most people suspect.

— Roseanne

This becomes doubly true for those of us who are working mothers. Early in 1995, *Newsweek* had a major cover story claiming one in four Americans is exhausted. I bet a remarkable percentage of those people were mothers of young children. Every working mother is doubly worn out by the time she gets to sleep at night. A working mother has two full-time jobs and will therefore be chronically tired for about eighteen years of her life. I know I was.

On the other hand, working can give us another center of strength, a relief from the constant demands of young children. Any way you cut it, being a mother is hard and tiring work. But I accepted the reality of perpetual exhaustion from day one. I knew I needed to give the girls all the time I could, so I simply slept less. I cut back on social obligations. I would arrange our schedule so that we did everything early. I'd need to have early dinners from time to time, curl up under my clean sheets, and read myself to sleep at nine o'clock. I cut back on many activities, sensing that since motherhood was opening new doors, some would have to be closed. But it was worth it, since for me, motherhood just enhanced all my abilities. I became more competent, more responsible, more alive and self-aware than ever before.

All we can do is our best to figure out what needs to be done as we go along. We'll never have it all worked out—that was true even *before* we had children!

Learning to Trust Your Instincts

I was twenty-six years old when I became a mother. I was unsure of myself. I lacked confidence and self-esteem and had little awareness of my own power. I was surrounded by authority figures, in my family and at work, who constantly tried to shape me up, make me over. I was particularly criticized for being a working mother. The office manager of the interior design firm where I worked wasn't subtle in letting me know that she thought that I should be home raising my children instead of working. My sister-in-law reprimanded me for my long working day.

We'd moved from uptown to midtown precisely to be only a few minutes' walk from my office. I made many sacrifices in order to be able to be a working mother, but I loved my work and I had to work to help put bread on the table. Believing my critics, however, I often found it difficult to trust my own instincts. I was insecure enough to allow myself to be bullied into agreeing with another's views just because the person was older and more assertive than I. I tended to survive by conforming, being "outer directed" in public, and keeping my true feelings to myself. But that all changed as I gained confidence as a mother.

When you become a mother, you have an unparalleled opportunity to learn to trust your heart. You may have had dif-

My first job is to be a good mother.

— Faye Dunaway

ficulty trusting your instincts before, but motherhood can teach you, little by little, to see that you have your own ideas, your own solutions to problems, your own rationales for what you do. You learn through experience what works for you and your child. If your two-year-old throws herself on the floor because you tell her she cannot eat twenty cookies, you learn to trust that perhaps letting the tantrum play out is your best course with her. Listening to your own voice—without all the outside voices interfering—helps you make the right decisions for your child as well as for yourself.

> *Little children are still the symbol of the eternal marriage between love and duty.*
>
> *— George Eliot*

I was helped to hear my own voice by listening to my girls' voices. They honestly expressed their needs. If they were hungry, we would eat. Who cares whether it's lunchtime or not? If they wanted to be with me, I was there. If they wanted to be alone to daydream, I was out of sight. By relaxing into this reciprocity, we exchanged rights and privileges. Alexandra and Brooke became *my* teachers, and in turn, I taught them that there *are* adults who listen to children, who take them seriously, and who find their company stimulating and exhilarating.

> *I saw pure love when my son looked at me, and I knew that I had to make a good life for the two of us.*
>
> *— Suzanne Somers*

Another area where mothers can sharpen their instincts is in learning to set limits and in fostering a sense of structure. Most mothers would agree that they raise happier and healthier children when their children know what they can and cannot do. When a child knows that crying and screaming will not get her what she wants, she learns to compromise. She also learns how to tolerate frustration and disappointment, both of which will be inevitable throughout her life. Children don't really want to have the last word. Emotionally, it's like putting a two-year-old behind a steering wheel and telling him to drive.

A mother learns to trust her own authority; sometimes she's just got to say no because she's the mother. When a mother grows confident in her intentions and in her abilities, she's able to set limits in a way that is comfortable for everybody.

Earth's crammed with heaven.

— Elizabeth Barrett Browning

I am a big believer, though, in breaking the rules, selectively—particularly when it comes to bedtimes. If you're unable to be with your children during the day because of work or because you were away on a business trip, you have to make adjustments in their schedule. Many times I would feel perfectly justified in keeping my daughters up late because either their father or I (or both) had been away. We knew we needed time to be together.

A single event can awaken within us a stranger totally unknown to us. To live is to be slowly born.

— Antoine de Saint-Exupéry

When you develop this trust in yourself, you will have a greater sense of when you need to be strict and when you can loosen your control.

With self-trust comes mindfulness and the ability to be a good and fair negotiator with children. You learn to wield your power with consideration because you recognize how little power your "opponent" has. Children grow through testing the temperature of the water and by driving a hard bargain. But you, as the final arbiter, must use your authority for your mutual benefit. Children can be manipulative, but until they learn other skills,

manipulation is the only instrument they have. You must judge when and how to accommodate them. This may demand that you rise above your need to control and have the final say. Knowing when to stand firm and when to let go comes from trusting yourself. My faith and trust in my own instincts has expanded throughout my life as a mother.

Efficiency Goes Out the Window

Before we became mothers, most of us learned a good deal about time management; we learned how to be efficient in all of our work. We'd fly into goal-oriented projects, carrying around a list of chores and crossing them off one by one until they were all completed. Those days are over. Certainly, the skills we acquired by being more organized and capable come in handy in motherhood. But if we mothers whirl around expecting to get the same sense of completion from our tasks, we're doomed to frustration.

I've got a woman's ability to stick to a job and get on with it when everyone else walks off and leaves it.

— Margaret Thatcher

To survive and thrive, a mother must learn to let some things go. A mother in full swing can be an awe-inspiring sight, having more hands than an octopus. But sometimes, something's got to give. Yes, we do have days when we've simply got to reach out in all directions. One hand rubs a child's aching tummy while the other flips pancakes on a griddle, sorts the mail, does another load of dishes, folds laundry, administers first aid. And many mothers also have full-time jobs outside the home on top

When people ask me what I do, I always say I am a mother first. Your children represent your thoughts. Your children are a statement.

— Jacqueline Jackson

of it all. Indeed, there are times when as a mother you feel like a magical "can do" person. But watch out; there are limits to how long you can keep it up. Sometimes you "can do," but at other times you must accept that you simply cannot.

Motherhood teaches a more fulfilling lesson: You don't have to do it all. You can be a better mother without all that overachieving. There are occasions when it is essential to do only one thing at a time: when you are reading your child a book; when you are listening to her speak; when you and your family are preparing dinner. The key to being a good and happy mother is to allow yourself to be fully present and to know when your undivided attention is called for. I've never regretted walking away from a frenetic work pace to escape with one daughter to a quiet, private place, where I could hold her on my lap, wrap my arms around her, and whisper, "Oh, how I love you."

I recall doing this for Alexandra when she was crying about her best friend having chicken pox and missing their sleep-over date, or when Brooke realized she had lost her favorite beaded bracelet on a trip to the zoo. I had to take time to help them and to understand their disappointments.

Before your children were born, you may have hung on tightly to your sense of control, but when they arrive you realize that the need to have control is controlling you. Mothers have to learn to roll with the punches. If you've never been able to do it before, here's your chance!

Think of your children as works in progress, sometimes taking awkward and disturbing shapes. They're not savages who must be kept under control. They don't always know what they're doing; they're trying to figure things out for the first time. Naturally, then, they're going to do a lot that is wrong or bothersome. That's how they learn. When you are fully involved in this becoming process, you help your children understand not only what they must do, but why it's right to do so. When you get angry at your child for spilling the milk and breaking the dishes, it's not the same as getting angry with your husband for throwing his dirty socks on the floor. He should know better. But children are just discovering the difference between accidents and deliberate misbehaving. Often, they're not such willing students. Nevertheless, as a mother your job is to help them along this path of learning, understanding that they often know not what they do.

In the sheltered simplicity of the first days after a baby is born, one sees again the magical closed circle. The miraculous sense of two people existing only for each other.

— Anne Morrow Lindbergh

Children, as miraculous and wonderful as they are, get into things they're not supposed to; they do things you expressly tell them not to do. They break a piece of your favorite china while having a tea party. They draw on the walls, spill food, leave their chocolate fingerprints on your chintz sofa, and play manicurist with your fire-engine red nail polish on your bright-white bedspread. While they're spray painting you a Valentine's Day card, the red paint gets all over your entrance hall.

I'm Zen cool as a rule, but I didn't always find it easy to roll with the punches. I remember one Saturday afternoon when Brooke was only a year old, she decided she wanted to sit in a bowl of cooked rice on the kitchen floor, and fling the rice with a spoon in all directions — including the ceiling. I couldn't believe it. Within a few minutes she was out of control. I slipped and fell on the greasy floor. Rather than getting upset, she and I laughed and giggled. I understood that she was just having fun. And I wanted her to have fun. We pretended we were sitting on the beach playing with the sand. I captured this moment of pure joy with a picture to show her when she got older and could appreciate seeing how happy she was.

I'm reminded of a sweet story told to me by my friend Melanie Petro:

I was talking with one of my neighborhood playmates from grade school this past summer when she asked: "How is your sweet mother?"

"Great," I replied.

"Melanie, you have the sweetest mother. I was thinking about her the other day, because I remembered walking to your house one day with my mother when we were in the first or second grade, and there were hundreds of napkins all over the floor, on the table, the stove, and in the drawers. My mother asked your mother what had happened, and your mother just smiled and said, 'Melanie wanted to play with the napkins.'"

To show a child what has once delighted you, to find the child's delight added to your own, so that there is now a double delight seen in the glow of trust and affection, this is happiness.

— J. B. Priestley

Mothers are instrumental in helping children formulate their character and values, which demands that we be understanding and patient—not to mention having a good sense of humor.

Mothers also can't keep a tight schedule. Trying to keep a strict schedule could be devastating in the long run. The penetrating truth of motherhood, which we learn anew every day, is that no matter how accustomed we are to having our own way, our way is now something we must negotiate with this vital, lively, demanding human being whose very powerlessness forces us to make ourselves consider things from his or her perspective. I had to deal with this whenever I encountered my daughters' messy rooms. Can you imagine an interior decorator who cannot keep her house clean? When I'd go to de-thug the girls' rooms with them, I'd enter into this assignment as a necessary task, thinking, *How could I have raised such slobs?* When I was a child, I had to bounce quarters on my bed after I made it to be sure it had been done correctly. I wasn't allowed to live in a pig sty. But with the girls, despite the tornado that hit their room time and again, we'd always end up laughing hysterically.

When we can relate to our children with this openness, we will grow and become, along with our children, more relaxed, flexible, and humane beings. Our children can give us an awareness of immediacy. They teach us how to become absorbed in the moment, rather than be tyrannized by schedules. This arouses us into living profoundly, rather than keeping up outward appearances. Relating to our children is living reality. How we react is key. Being effective is far nobler than being perfect. Perfectionism has no place in motherhood.

> *When you are a mother, you are never really alone in your thoughts. You are connected to your child and to all those who touch your lives. A mother always has to think twice, once for herself and once for her child.*
>
> *— Sophia Loren*

Learning from Our Children

You have the potential to learn so much when you become a mother. One of the things I'm most aware of learning was how to speak to Alexandra and Brooke. I remember a period of time when I was getting up at five o'clock, writing, bathing the girls, dressing and feeding them, and sending them off to school as I went off to work. Often my patience was severely tested on those hectic mornings. Every day had its moments of strain. I had to become extra-aware of my mood to prevent myself from overreacting to my girls or ordering them to do something — which I did do on occasion. I finally learned the balance between being firm and being flexible. They heard me a lot better when I achieved this balance.

No commitment in this whole world demands quite as much as bringing up children.

— Janene Wolsey Baadsgaard

If you tend to say what's on your mind rather than considering the impact of your words on another; if you are impatient when explaining something; if you give orders rather than ask for help; if you express yourself urgently rather than calmly — you're probably going to suffer unnecessary miscommunication, and as a result, pain and frustration in dealing with your children. If you really want to communicate, and if you want your children to hear you, you'll soon learn to speak so that your children can really listen. We have more of an impact when the tone of our voice is tender and loving, especially in profoundly serious moments. There are certainly times in our lives when we're edgy or anxious for one reason or another. We're not always at our best. Sometimes we slip off our path. Some of the stupidest things have flown out of my mouth in such moments.

I'm grateful, though, for two words I continuously taught my girls: *I'm sorry.* Sometimes I'd tell them why I was off my beam, and other times those reasons were too private or troublesome for their young ears. Basically, I was a softy, even though I had my outbursts. I was mindful of them and wanted them to learn how to cope in either situation.

Not only does our relationship with our children teach us how to communicate better, but it also helps us learn how to enjoy time together — even in close quarters. I loved seeing how many ways we could resolve the problems that come from living in close quarters. When there isn't any static between us, the flow of communication is open and authentic. When the girls were little, we had "quiet time." Each of us could read or rest, play or putter independently for specific periods of time, as long as we didn't disturb the peace for another. The girls often wanted to curl up in my bed, which was fine. You can and do learn from your children principles and techniques for living well together.

> *Making the decision to have a child—it's momentous. It is to decide forever to have your heart go walking around outside your body.*
>
> *— Elizabeth Stone*

Empathy and Respect for Process

Children enormously expand our ability to empathize with others and to see things from another's point of view. Mothering children also teaches us to have faith in the growth process and in life itself. This, in a sense, is the promise we make when we become mothers. We promise to try our best to understand our children as separate beings learning to make their own way in the world. Human beings are the only species that can consciously make such promises. I made a covenant with my daughters that I would always be available to them, but that I would always try to respect their independence and their opinions. Our children are separate beings, not simply extensions of ourselves.

I confronted this head-on when Brooke revealed to me, just after graduating from high school, that she wanted to live in Paris. She persuaded me that she shouldn't even apply for college. This was not what I expected to hear. I received calls from everyone, including her private day school, pressuring me (in patronizing tones) to force her to go to college: "It isn't fair to Brooke not to push her to apply."

I love these little people; and it is not a slight thing, when they, who are so fresh from God, love us.

— Charles Dickens

I stuck by Brooke. After all, I hadn't gone to college. As it happened, serendipity intervened. A lifelong friend invited her to spend a weekend at Denison University in Granville, Ohio, to watch her brother perform in a play. I happened to be giving a lecture in a museum nearby. On Sunday, when I tried to pry her away from campus to catch a plane back to New York, she whispered to me, "I'm coming here to college." And she did.

After Brooke graduated, she bolted to Paris and lived there for a year, until an editor called her and begged her to come to work for her in New York. Things worked out well, but even so, I believed in Brooke's feelings, trusting she would do what was right for her—not for me or her school—and, in doing so, she helped us all to grow.

I always try to be respectful of Alexandra and Brooke's decision-making abilities. I remember when Alexandra was a teenager and first started going to discotheques. Peter and I would wait up for her, paralyzed with fear, reading in the living room, waiting to hear the door open and see that she was safe. We'd kiss goodnight and smell the nicotine in her hair and on her clothes, and imagine the den of iniquity she'd spent the evening in.

On one particular Saturday night Alexandra received a phone call from a friend and classmate begging for help. "Alexandra," she pleaded, "come help me. I've been dancing and I had too much to drink. I've just thrown up in the ladies' room. I'm too weak and disoriented to get home alone."

Hearing this, Alexandra (Mother Teresa) climbed out of her bed, put on a pair of jeans, and took a taxi down to Studio 54. There she found her friend, pale and weak. Arm in arm they went outside and grabbed a taxi back to the friend's house, where Alexandra fed her ginger ale and saltines, put her to bed, and returned home—only to find that she'd been locked out of the house. Meanwhile, I hadn't been able to get to sleep that night. About an hour after Alexandra went to bed, I padded to the kitchen to get some grapefruit juice. When I walked past Alexandra's room I found the door open, and I could see from the covers that she was in bed. "I love you, darling," I called out. Silence. This didn't make sense. She couldn't be asleep already! So I walked into her room and noticed that her pillows were propping up the covers, not Alexandra. She was gone.

When Alexandra was forced to ring the doorbell because she was locked out, we had to talk. She pleaded with us to listen to her side of the story. She hadn't wanted to disturb us; she'd done what she had to do for a close friend. And she was safe. By the end of our

> Every child comes with the message that God is not yet discouraged of man.
>
> — Rabindranath Tagore

> All I have seen teaches me to trust the Creator for all I have not seen.
>
> — Emerson

long discussion, I recognized Alexandra as a rescuer. Whenever a friend's in need, she's there. Time and again, even after all these years, I'm impressed with how she acted on a higher power that night, even if it worried me to pieces.

When you live for love alone, you become filled with love, & that is to be a saint.

— Thomas Merton

Our children help us to have faith in life's processes. Becoming mothers teaches us everything about respect for life. I've found, as the mother of two daughters, that the love I feel for them fills me with my best self. This "I-thou" space between us is mutually nourishing. Our souls are elevated to a place where we have more understanding, more grace. Because my commitment to them is a promise that I will be trustworthy, I become that trustworthy person and experience for myself new levels of love and understanding.

Children inspire us to love because they give so much of it themselves. Children believe us to be beautiful because of their love for us, and this love they shower on us helps us to be lovely at the core. I wanted to be everything I could be for my daughters. But not only did I want to be this reservoir of sensitivity and compassion, I also wanted to show my girls that I was capable of hammering things together. I wanted them to respect me and themselves for *all* our many great qualities and capabilities.

Renewal

Motherhood transforms us, not once, but over and over again. When our children are infants, we become baby nurses and experts on nutrition and early child development. At first, we may be terrified at how little we know. When I was breast-feeding Alexandra, she'd finish nursing and begin crying immediately. I was convinced that my milk was drying up and that I was actually starving her. A few conversations with a doctor cleared that up. But there were always worries and fears. What about those high fevers? Will they roll over on time? Grow the right amount of hair? Ever learn to talk? At first, everything seems to us a cause for grave concern. Little by little, we bear up under these strains and learn to admit our fears and surmount them. We get smarter about what really matters because we learn that we will survive whatever we must. And we learn that it is absolutely essential that we do our best but also that we relax, both for our own sake and for our children's. When the baby stops crying because of something we've fixed, we can relax and become more accustomed to these natural ebbs and flows of crises. In life, things are always in flux.

When we voice, then, the necessity of setting the feminine spirit utterly and absolutely free, thought turns naturally not to rights of the woman, nor indeed of the mother, but to the rights of the child—of all children in the world.

— Margaret Sanger

This theme recurs throughout our lives as mothers. We feel we'll barely survive the tortures of chasing our toddlers away from dangerous-looking glass coffee tables. We worry a little too much about their shyness or their aggressiveness in the sandbox. But when we see them survive the near collisions, and watch them learn to share with their friends—in between fights— we experience this sense of renewal, and our confidence is restored as we watch them learn to survive in their own way.

As our babies grow into children, we are called upon to be

a fountain of knowledge, providing the key to the storehouse of all of life's facts and mysteries. Suddenly, we must present ourselves as experts in the naming of whales and dinosaurs. Not only that—we must know all identifying characteristics: which are carnivores, which herbivores, which might live in the ocean we may be riding on when we take a spin in a boat, and whether or not we'll be safe. Then we must be math experts, add to that computers (about which most of our children know a lot more than we). I have a friend who brushed up on her rusty French so she could converse with her eleven-year-old son at the dinner table.

Later, our faith is tested as we are called upon to help our maturing adolescents bridge the sometimes terrifying divide between childhood and a burgeoning maturity. We sometimes have to watch helplessly as our children encounter the fear of testing themselves in the world on their own. No mother is alone in feeling perplexed at her adolescent's behavior in these sometimes emotionally turbulent times. There will be falls, but now they're not from bicycles. There could be trouble at school, eating disorders, problems with sex or drugs, or even with the law. But we can remain calm, and flow into each situation with a loving heart. Here again, we witness the ebb and flow of crises, but now, perhaps, we can remain calm as we remember how we rose to the challenge during many of the other challenging passes.

We also learn the difficult lesson that we

> *Giving birth generates a flood of powerful hormones, generating a surge of energy pouring through the body. In a woman with healthy memories of her early childhood, this surging energy is experienced as a strong bond to her child.*
>
> — *Dr. Deepak Chopra*

cannot protect our children from making their own mistakes. We cannot prevent them from encountering the hardships that life hands out, sometimes seemingly at random. But our trust in our children helps them learn to trust themselves to make good judgment calls. After a time, we worry less and less as we watch them become more and more competent.

When I was in Jackson, Mississippi, talking to some high school students, many of them confided to me how they hated many adults' assumptions that they were always up to no good.

When we have confidence in our children, we support their best impulses, and this helps them thrive. We are not in charge of our children's life course. We want them to be happy. But we must understand that our path will not be theirs. When we anticipate the best, we are rarely let down.

We constantly must check ourselves, particularly during the difficult turns of adolescence, to make sure we remain open and understanding—even in the most difficult circumstances. We can take courage when difficult times come by reflecting on the many turning points we feared we'd never survive, but did.

The pendulum swings continuously. This principle reappears throughout your life as a parent, teaching you essential lessons about what it means to be alive, moment to moment, in the process of change and becoming. Our children grow so rapidly, physically, mentally, and emotionally, reminding us that we are never fixed, static creatures, but are always capable of stretching ourselves to reach our own full potential,

> *All mothers are rich when they love their children. There are no poor mothers, no ugly ones, no old ones. Their love is always the most beautiful of joys.*
>
> *— Maurice Maeterlinck*

growing in awareness about life, about ourselves, about responsibility and the commitment to be more fully alive.

Our capacity to remain flexible, to stretch ourselves for our children, ultimately transforms us. And our children inspire and encourage us through their ability to learn and change, to keep the muscle that controls flexibility limber and alive. Babies and children don't make us complete, but their life struggles, their curiosity, and their resilience, are so inspiring that they encourage us to be more and to believe more in life itself.

Growing in Tough Times

One of the most painful transformations I underwent with my children occurred while watching Brooke suffer the death of her best friend, Courtney Steel, who was brutally murdered by a hit-and-run drunk driver. I never experienced greater pain in my life than seeing my seventeen-year-old daughter grieving so deeply. Brooke would stay in her bedroom behind the closed door, and I'd be in mine, next door. We were separate but together. I felt I was supporting her in her pain by being close by, but not smothering her. I read many books about death and with Brooke had experienced many parallel dreams about Courtney.

...touch our own upper limit and live in our own highest center of energy....

— William James

One afternoon, I felt Brooke was drowning in her grief. Maybe I felt that way because I was. I asked her to come into the kitchen. There at the table we had an exchange charged with love, pain, anxiety, tenderness, thoughts of death—the whole spectrum of emotional energy. We screamed, we yelled, and we cried until we wailed. We'd grab ice from the freezer and put it into dish towels to rest on our eyes. But we also laughed through our hysterical pain. "We don't want to scare anyone!" I said. A mutual friend of ours happened to be in the apartment that afternoon photographing my bedroom closet for *Redbook* magazine. Suddenly the photographer's lights

> *If you judge people, you have no time to love them.*
>
> — *Mother Teresa*

caught fire. They called 911 and a team of fire fighters came with hoses to put out the fire while Brooke and I thrashed out our painful passage from accepting Courtney's tragic death, to letting go and moving on.

During that sad, painful time, a friend kept urging me to get my mind off the sadness I felt for what Brooke was going through. But I didn't want to escape the hurt. I wanted to be there for her. Because we stuck it out together, we were on the same emotional wavelength and were able to help each other during this tragic crisis. The bond was solid. I'd never felt more stretched in my life.

Most mothers agree, we'd gladly take on our children's pain if we thought we could spare them. But reality teaches us that there are no shortcuts through painful situations. As mothers we learn to respect this limitation. Each individual soul has to encounter experience and see it through personally. Life must affect us all.

Deepening Our Stake in Life

When we become mothers, we feel a greater stake in life. We grow tremendously in our insight and knowledge of human nature and the ways of the world. As our children get older, we may take an even greater interest in politics and in the society in which our children are growing up, appreciating how deeply they are being affected by it all. Everything and everyone in the world becomes of critical importance to mothers because everything affects our children's lives, now and in their future. Our relationship to everything and everyone, both private and public, becomes more relevant and more essential.

Of all that is wonderful in the human being, our most glorious asset is this capacity to change ourselves.

– Eknath Easwaran

When you become a mother, you want to give and do everything for your child. That includes wanting them to have a wide network of support. You want them to know many wonderful people, both in your family and in your social world. Having a child can transform your relationship to family, sometimes in wonderful ways. I found I took a far greater interest in family stories, myths, and legends that had been passed along over the years. Once I gave birth to Alexandra and Brooke, I experienced an enormous capacity to connect with beloved family members, because of the wonderful effect they were having on my daughters. This in turn helped me have closer, warmer, more real encounters with them as well. I also loved sharing family life with friends, those who had children and those who didn't. When you consider it, so much energy and so many resources are needed to raise a child, it seems absurd that it only be done by the parents alone. I think we all need each other a lot more when we become mothers.

As parents, we also become more mindful of the social forces that affect our children's lives. The limited availability of good child care in this country points toward a terrible lack of concern for the well-being of our children. What could be more important to a parent than knowing there are provisions for day care, for safe streets, good schools, and good health care for our children? When you become a mother, suddenly the state of the world becomes of paramount importance. When Alexandra had pneumonia as a little girl and lay in an oxygen tent at Lenox Hill Hospital in New York, I had plenty of time to stare at the grim walls that very sick children had to live within. I decided to do something about it by placing colorful banners and other decorations in the dismal corridors and rooms. I also volunteered to create a lively, colorful environment at another facility, the children's wing of Columbia Presbyterian Hospital. I also joined a nonprofit organization's board of trustees to help shelter the homeless and provide soup kitchens in schools and churches, and I became more active in our church, wanting to ensure good leadership for the next generation.

Make yourself familiar with the angels, and behold them frequently in spirit; for, without being seen, they are present in you.

— St. Francis de Sales

Children Bring You Love

When my children were born, I felt I was participating in a rare, precious interrelationship. I felt myself being replenished by my concern, trust, and faith in them. The more I believed in them, the greater freedom I had to raise my sights for myself. I felt exhilarated watching the growth and expansion of my children's world through my tenderness and care.

Children transform us because loving them increases our

ability to love—both to give and to receive. So many readers tell me that since having their children they have become finer, kinder, more caring people. It doesn't really matter who you were before you became a mother; you might have been cold, remote, and angry. Once you become a mother, you open up a little more. I believe that motherhood offers us a kind of poetic vision of life. And like the poet, whose every sense is tuned into the world to find something beautiful or true about life, we mothers are attuned to what our children need to be happy and to thrive.

Because I am a mother, I am incapable of being shocked: as I never was when I was not one.

— Margaret Atwood

"Teaching is the perpetual end and office of all things," Emerson assures us. "Teaching, instruction is the main design that shines through the sky and earth." When we become mothers, we see the world as an opportunity to educate ourselves for our own and for our children's sake. All the great lessons I've learned have been from my Zen masters, Alexandra and Brooke. Through them I learned to be more open to love.

Most mothers are instinctive philosophers.

— Harriet Beecher Stowe

Recently, I was sitting on a beach on an island escape when a three-year-old came right up to me and placed a kiss on my cheek. She must have sensed my love of children. She was an angel connecting me back to my girls. Children allow us to be ourselves. They respond to our love without criticism. They aren't trying to impress others. Their pure, honest, heartfelt feelings and their immediate relationships with others are what matter to them most.

In our somewhat cynical age, it is redeeming to see that children always recognize our tenderness, our vulnerability, our longing to be accepted for who we truly are. Children transform us because they teach us what's true and real, what's worthwhile. Whenever we are in the presence of a loving child, we are transported into a passionate and vital world. There we experience the deeper and more acute perceptions of the mystery and the miracle of existence. Through that experience, we know that in some subtle way children hold the secret to happiness. As we become enlarged by them, we cherish our ability to become wide open to an ever expanding ability to love.

> *You will see the divinity in every creature.*
>
> *— Bhagavad Gita*

Chapter 3

What Does a Mother Do for Her Children?

"You love me more than love."

—Alexandra Brandon Stoddard, age six,
January 31, 1973

What does a mother do for her child? She changes 4,380 diapers, leaving a few for Dad. She gets awakened 1,625 times from sleep. She prepares 2,920 bottles of milk and juice. She plays hide-and-seek 730 times. She gives her child 2,555 baths, knowing her child could use about 10,555 more due to perpetual stickiness. She will pick up and hold her child 91,250 times—maybe two children at once—equaling 95 pounds of clinging joy. She will clean up after her child 40,150 times, smiling at her little one's industriousness.

By the time a child reaches the age of twelve, a mother has made 4,015 peanut butter sandwiches, wiped up 16,420 spills, sung 10,950 songs, said prayers 12,700 times, and read 8,760 books, some as many as 87 times each. My mother read me *The Little Engine That Could* so many times that *I* held the book because she had memorized every word.

How many times did the girls want me to

Who ran to help me when I fell, and would some pretty story tell, or kiss the place to make it well? My mother.

— Jane Taylor

read Peggy Parrish's *Amelia Bedelia*, or A.A. Milne's *Winnie the Pooh*, or Albert Lamorisse's *The Red Balloon*, or Dr. Seuss's *Oh, the Places You'll Go!*

> *The mother's heart is the child's schoolroom.*
>
> — Henry Ward Beecher

A mother will hug her child 46,720 times, kiss him 17,520 times, and give 116,800 love pats. She will say, "I love you" to her child at least 21,900 times, and always wish she said it more often. I know this because I'm a mother. A mother will do anything for her children because her commitment and her love are infinite.

I wonder how long the list would really be if it took in *everything* a mother does for her children? A mother loves her children without setting conditions for that love, while at the same time she gently sets limits to help children learn to adapt and compromise. A mother offers support and understanding even as she teaches her children how to hear the word *no*. Mother is the keeper of the hearth, yet in order to spend meaningful time with her children, she sometimes has to stop that work before she runs herself into the ground. A mother delights in playing with her children and develops the sensitivity to take whatever opportunities arise for a quiet, loving conversation. A mother constantly reaches inside herself to share and show what is good and positive in the world, even though there is pain and disappointment to acknowledge, too. A mother instills values in her children not only by telling them what is right but by being a living example of what is right. A mother provides stability by making a

> *I am sorry to say that Peter was not very well during the evening. His mother put him to bed, and made some camomile tea; and she gave a dose of it to Peter!*
>
> — Beatrix Potter

child's world feel safe, yet she must allow for flexibility to make a child's world fun.

What a mother is saying to her child with that touch is "Live."

— Dr. Rachel Naomi Remen

As mothers, we do whatever needs to be done for each child, at the time. We face the awkward times, handling public temper tantrums and meetings in the principal's office. We accept the inconvenient, rocking our children to sleep in the middle of the night and racing out of work early to take our children to the doctor. I'll never forget the pain I felt when I came home from the office one afternoon to learn that the baby-sitter had taken Alexandra to Dr. Davies to remove a big splinter. I regretted not having been there to hold her hand and kiss her, wiping away her tears. We also deal with the unpleasant, cleaning up the mess after a child projectile vomits in bed all over the wall and floor, including the toy box.

To love is to receive a glimpse of heaven.

— Karen Sunde

Somehow, regardless of how tough a situation is, when it comes to our children, we're there 300 percent, rolling with the punches, keeping our sense of humor, and, in countless ways, showing our children all the good in the world. But most of all, a mother never gives up on her children.

The Gift of Unconditional Love

What our children need from us most and what we try to give them most abundantly is our unconditional love. Our unconditional love gives our child a system of support they are unlikely to find anywhere else in their lives, with the exception only of their closest friends and important lovers in later life. Still, a parent's unconditional love is a unique energy. It is pure love given in an unusual generosity. When children have this loving safety net, when they know that whatever happens they can turn to mother for comfort, strength, and understanding, they will grow up to be centered, strong, and loving adults. The more a mother makes available her unconditional support for her children's being, the greater the children's chances are to reach full potential.

Trust yourself. You know more than you think you do.

— Dr. Benjamin Spock

I was moved and impressed in a recent talk I had with Carol, a waitress in Noah's restaurant in Stonington Village. One of her three children, Jason, is a part-time dishwasher there. Carol loves her children unabashedly and we often talk about how much fun it is being a mom. "My kids are great. Who knows, Alexandra, one just might be president of the United States. I think it will be my daughter, Amanda. Yeah." With a huge grin and a double thumbs up, Carol nods her head. "Yeah, it's about time. I can't do enough for my kids. They're my whole life."

Carol's bursting enthusiasm and belief in her children is going to give them a very special edge. Who knows how much this love will determine their future happiness and abilities? I tend to think, quite a lot.

I love my children from this abundance, for who they are, not from a need for them to be any particular way. Not everyone agrees on this wholehearted support for children. Some say it spoils the child. I've been to lectures given by psychologists who believe that giving this unmitigated love and support doesn't prepare children for the real world where they will not be so encouraged. But the real world is cold. We counteract by providing our love. The outside world is not always a very good judge of individual strength and ability—you either fit the mold or you get chucked out. It's a parent's job to help a child discover her own particular strengths so that she will go out into the world bolstered by this knowledge. Spoiling a child is another matter entirely; it has nothing to do with being your child's greatest fan. Indulging your child in his bad habits and failing to teach your child that there are limits to his demands can contribute to a child's difficulty in later life. But love? You can never give a child too much love and support. Never.

I remember a touching letter I received from one reader whose mother's support helped her to believe in herself. It read:

At age six, I decided that I wanted to become an actress. While my father just assumed it was a little girl's dream that would eventually disappear, my mother, a physical therapist, always took me seriously and encouraged me in even the smallest ways. She was the audience when I put on plays with my friends. She always helped me put the costumes together. Throughout high school and college she remained enthusiastic about my acting, even flying more than a thousand miles to see me in a play. Presently, I am waitressing in New York and attending close to ten auditions a week. Mom is still my biggest supporter.

God knows that a mother needs fortitude and courage and tolerance and flexibility and patience and firmness and nearly every other brave aspect of the human soul. But because I happen to be a parent of almost fiercely maternal nature, I praise casualness. It seems to me the rarest of virtues. It is useful enough when children are small. It is important to the point of necessity when they are adolescents.

—Phyllis McGinley

> *What do girls do who haven't any mothers to help them through their troubles?*
>
> — *Louisa May Alcott*

Children are born with self-love. It's up to us to keep this love alive. We do so by applauding our children's accomplishments. When we love our children, we come to know their strengths. In turn, they learn to value their strengths.

We can also support our children by helping them find ways to express and respect their sensitivities. If you have a painfully shy child, instead of pressuring her to be more social, encourage her to pursue her interests. You can help by doing some of her favorite activities with her. Whether she loves animals or collecting stamps, your soft, gentle, loving energy has a mysterious way of melting away her shyness. Gradually, she's less afraid.

Some children need help managing their aggressiveness. One five-year-old boy was so wound up, he'd punch his mother and his teacher in the face. His mother came up with a brilliant solution. She got him a pair of boxing gloves and a punching bag. She even bought herself a pair of boxing gloves so that they could box together. He liked the idea and it cured his behavior.

It's not always easy to express your unconditional love. Many things happen throughout the day that try your patience and understanding. Perhaps your child refuses to take a nap, fights over a plastic toy bus with a sibling, or cuts up your favorite tablecloth in order to make dolls' clothes. Maybe he takes a cupful of freshly sharpened pencils off your desk and, with the point toward you, charges as though bullfighting in Madrid. Or maybe she eats too many sweets and is thrown into a sugar-induced rampage. Our perspective narrows to one of frustration and we're not amused. It is easy to love a newborn baby unconditionally, or a toddler, or a sweet five-year-old — even though he may keep you up all night, or run you down into exhaustion. Babies and young children are naturally lovable, by necessity. If nature hadn't arranged it that way, how would we survive the shrieking and the twenty-four hours of constant attention?

As a child passes through all the different and increasingly demanding stages of development, our patience may be tested, but never our unconditional love. The love *never* disappears. It is the very force that brings things together, through divine grace. So, a mother's unconditional love, by definition, cannot be tested. This is our spiritual energy at work, always loving our child even if we don't like what he's up to at the moment.

A child's need for a mother's love "no matter what" deepens during the more difficult periods because of an innate trust in their bond. First, we had to make sure we made the peanut butter and jelly sandwiches with just the right ratio of peanut butter to jelly. Later, things get more unnerving. Whatever the rebellion, however the style of the hair or condition of the jeans, however long the mysterious silences or the unpredictable anger, we know in our hearts that we can weather any storm because we know not only that it will pass, but that our unwavering support will see us all through. Giving that support actually enlarges a mother's love, and bolsters her faith that everything will be OK.

> *Kind words can be short and easy to speak, but their echoes are truly endless.*
>
> *— Mother Teresa*

In the final analysis, if you treat children as if they were what they should be, you help them to become themselves. And that's the best person they can be. William James reminds us, "If an Emerson were forced to be a Wesley, or a Moody forced to be a Whitman, the total human consciousness of the divine would suffer." My mother dressed my sister and me alike as children, but that was only a cosmetic similarity. We were as different as two people can be. As William James taught his students:

> No two of us have identical difficulties, nor should we be expected to work out identical solutions. Each, from his peculiar angle of observation, takes in a certain sphere of fact and trouble, which each must deal with in a unique manner. One of us must soften himself, another must harden himself; one must yield a point, another must stand firm—in order to better defend the position assigned him....The divine can mean no single quality, it must mean a group of qualities, by being champions of which in alternation, different men may all find worthy missions. Each attitude being a syllable in human nature's total message, it takes the whole of us to spell the meaning out completely.

A mother is the truest friend we have when trials, heavy and sudden, fall upon us; when adversity takes the place of prosperity.

— Washington Irving

A friend's daughter once shared with me her memories of being intensely introverted as a teenager. "Alexandra," she said, "my reclusion began at the height of my adolescent insecurity, a time when I was absolutely awful to my mother. I would come home from high school and go straight to my room and shut the door, barely saying 'hello' to Mom. This went on for close to a year. Looking back, I know her feelings must have been very hurt by my actions, but she never showed it. Instead she let me have my space, which I think is what I really needed. She never forced me to talk. She never became angry at my constant bitterness. But she was always available for me and I always felt this. She knew intuitively that when I was ready, I would be receptive to her love."

It seems to me I spent my life in car pools, but you know, that's how I kept track of what was going on.

— Barbara Bush

Love of our children can never be founded on who or what we would like them to be. Our love must be based on who they are, or else it is not love for them. It's not always easy to understand your children's needs—they are complicated little beings and they are each so different from the other. Discovering who your child is is a lifelong process. But as spiritual leader Eric Butterworth reminds us so eloquently, "the tulip is a tulip even when it is nothing but a dry and shriveled bulb. The egg is a bird. The acorn is an oak tree....The finished work does not require a great will to make it, but the willingness to let it unfold." A mother's mindfulness, her attentiveness to her children, and her availability for whatever may come are what make love and understanding possible.

This does not necessarily mean that a mother can never be too busy or too caught up in other things. We can only do so much at one time. The essential thing is that when a mother is available, she's there for her child with acceptance and without judgment. As mothers, we are not charged with making over our child, but with letting their divine light shine through. We are there as their fundamental foundation, enabling them to become, to grow, to make mistakes, to transform, and to deepen.

There are hidden opportunities in life to show your unconditional love. When a mother relinquishes expectations of reward or appreciation because her caring acts are complete in themselves, her loving energy flows more freely. Giving love to our children increases our energies. A mother's unconditional love teaches her child that though she may do something bad, she is inherently good. This faith enables a child to be herself, to fulfill her potential, and to step up to bat and send the ball soaring.

Keeper of the Hearth

Mothers can make home a haven. I love feeling a sense of domestic bliss; it's a feeling that wells up in the whole family when we are all together, yet doing our own thing, moving in and out of each other's landscape with grace and gratitude. One evening — not a particularly momentous evening, but an evening I remember with great pleasure — perfectly brings to life my idea of keeping the atmosphere of hearth and home balanced.

Peter was sitting in his favorite big, upholstered chair in his favorite "sweet spot" in the living room — where he can see everyone. He was reading some Henry James before dinner, but he was also watching everyone come and go. The girls were playing jacks on the kitchen floor. The apartment was perfumed by a roasting chicken and the sweet scent of several bunches of primroses and miniature daffodils which I had set out in gleaming brass and copper pots earlier in the day. The handle on one of the pots caught Peter's eye, which delighted

At present, our attitude toward teaching is too yang—too absolute, rational, and aggressive. What is needed is more yin— intuition, sensuousness, and subtlety— to bring back a delicate balance.

— Greta K. Nagel

him. I came to tell him about a letter I had received from my editor.

We sat together in this cheerful room for a few minutes until I disappeared to put the laundry away. When I reappeared, I had an armful of sheets, towels, and underwear; I looked like I had enough laundry for an army—or for a family at least twice our size. Out of the blue Peter just looked up at me and said, "Alexandra, I love you. Do you need any help?"

The applause of a single human being is of great consequence.

— Dr. Samuel Johnson

"No, thanks," I said. "I'm fine." Which I was, and I also knew Peter was trying to have a moment of peace. Peter loves observing family life (though he did have twinges of guilt sometimes at not always participating in the parade of domesticity while the girls were growing up). And I loved showing how well I could do it!

After putting the freshly laundered clothes away (I love the smell of fresh laundry), I returned to the kitchen, sat on the cork floor, and joined my girls in their game of jacks.

I loved filling my home with the sights, smells, and pleasures of domestic life for my children. But I also became mindful that the persistent kinetic action of housework without breaks can create tension. So, I always made sure that I took the time to sit down with the girls for a game of jacks, or whatever they were involved in.

Mothers are always there for you to listen, a shoulder to cry on, an ear, a voice.

— a cab driver from Toronto

One of the greatest gifts a mother can give to her child is a peaceful, serene atmosphere at home, and that includes enjoying each others' company quietly, between some motherly fussing about.

What Makes a Home Great for Children?

How can we make a home beautiful with children in mind? I learned a great deal about this from my mother, who was an interior decorator. She never gave my daughters toys to play with, but instead, gave them paint and wood samples, fabric swatches, and colored paper with colored pencils. They were encouraged, from the beginning, to use the stuff of the real world. I remember four-year-old Alexandra, when playing with a book of fabric samples, stating, "Ninnie, there's not a good pink in this whole book." My mother looked down from her desk at her granddaughter and, fascinated, joined Alexandra on the floor. Looking through the pink fabric samples together, she concluded, "Alexandra, darling, you're right. They're all *ugh.*"

Alexandra decorated her own room when she was four, and ever since, she and Brooke have given us advice and suggestions about our choice of colors and design. Once when I took Brooke to a client's apartment, she fell in love with the chartreuse rug in the living room and lay down on it, spreading her arms out like angel wings, delighting me, as well as the rug's proud owner. Early in my interior design career I realized what thrilled me then and continues to thrill me now: A child knows the difference between a house and a home. If a child feels comfortable in a room, chances are we adults will be happy there, too.

> The first, the most fundamental right of childhood is the right to be loved. The child comes into the world alone, defenseless, without resource. Only love can stand between his infant helplessness and the savagery of a harsh world.
>
> — Paul Hanly Furfey

One of my favorite rooms was designed largely by Tom, a nine-year-old boy who loves blue. Together we decorated his room with white walls, a blue ceiling, blue-and-white-striped cotton chintz curtains, and a bleached floor on which we placed a rag rug woven in eight different shades of blue and white. Everything we chose kept the room light and sparkling. Tom, his mother, and I bought a Van Gogh print — the one of a village with blue roofs — at the Metropolitan Museum of Art to hang over his daybed. Why is it, whenever I'm at his family's apartment, I love being in Tom's room? Children can be amazingly sensitive to what is beautiful. It's wonderful when mothers trust and enable their children to participate in the creative process.

> *In times of difficulty take refuge in compassion and truth.*
>
> — *Buddha*

When we have children, we should try to avoid decorating our homes with furniture that children can't touch. How does your home still express *you* while you are raising your children? You may hold back for a while on "fancy stuff" for safety's sake, but not everything nice is fragile. You can work creatively with your children. You don't have to worry about how you'll adjust to their ideas once you connect with their energy, you'll want to get into the act with them. Your spaces become more cheerful, more subjective, more intimate, more real, more *more* once you have children. The worst mistake you could make is to have your house appear to be a stage set where children must be quiet and sit still. Every room should be infused with the joyful spirit of family life. If a child lives in a house, I want to see that child in all his glory and creativity, I want to feel the presence of a young soul.

Be realistic, of course. It's fine to have certain areas you'd rather not have the children destroy — perhaps the living

For the mother is and must be, whether she knows it or not, the greatest, strongest and most lasting teacher her children have.

— Hannah Whitall Smith

room—but it's inappropriate to hang a CHILDREN KEEP OUT sign on the door of any room. It's just unrealistic to try to close off any rooms to children. Sure, I go a little crazy when the chocolate-covered ice-cream stick gets mushed into our yellow floral chintz sofa in the living room, or I discover a melted chocolate chip cookie under the cushion of a chair. But then I have to ask myself, what's important here?

What's important is to know your child, and make your home great for *all* of you. Far better to have the "living room" be true to its name where you, as a family, enjoy spending time living together. If you want a margin of control, you can always have a table set up in the kitchen where the children can eat, and make the living room off-limits to gooey food.

Keep furniture to a minimum in a child's place. Children need road space. Valuables should be hidden out of *sight*— merely out of reach is too tempting, and the consequences could be disastrous. Try to simplify, for a change. Our higher power teaches us that simplicity is supreme. Clean, crisp spaces provide space for children to play as well as peace of mind for us. Avoid the anxiety of trying to foresee what's going to be broken next. Bold, large-scale objects can be elegant, stylish, and practical.

Without hearts there is no home.

— Lord Byron

Really good upholstered furniture can't be hurt by child's play. Look for hand-tied springs if you're shopping for a couch; they can withstand happy children jumping for joy. Children like to play with furniture, making tents and campsites out of kitchen tables and chairs. You can limit "building" to their bedrooms and the kitchen. That way, children will know that there are reasonable boundaries. Whenever possible, participate in the construction, helping to fuel their creative energies. Have a "special" stack of blankets, comforters, and pillows in the linen closet on a low shelf, designed for use in "fort construction." What greater compliment to the "spirit of place" than to see a child build a new world under our noses? I believe it's an honor when children feel comfortable playing in our home.

> *What tigress is there that does not purr over her young ones, and fawn upon them in tenderness?*
>
> — St. Augustine

When my book *A Child's Place* was published in 1977, the photograph of Alexandra, Brooke, Peter's son Nathaniel and me on the back jacket was taken inside the children's closet, in front of a ladder leading to "A Secret Place." Here the children could go to escape the world or to play with friends, snuggling up to pillows, blankets, quilts, and all their fuzzy stuffed animals. This was a sanctuary for our daughters. Everyone needs spaces where we feel special.

> *...the readiness is all.*
>
> — William Shakespeare

Mother's Bosom Is the Kitchen

The kitchen is the living, breathing, active hub of the home. And, most often, mother is the one who keeps it alive and kicking. It's designed that way. What does a mother do to keep the hearth and make the kitchen a special place? I found it essential to have a kitchen table, not just a counter with chairs. I love sitting at our round table where we gather to have a snack, a talk, or a banquet, or to prepare a meal together.

The kitchen can be the working, creative center of the house, where many fun activities can be centered around food. The very things that disconcert the "sophisticated" adult are what amuses a mother who wants to delight her child. Making Jell-O in molds is always thrilling. Seeing the pure color and the way the shape pops out, fully formed, onto a platter always tickled the girls and me. For fun, you can try smearing a plastic tray with whipped cream and spelling out your child's name in blueberries. Presentation, not nutrition or quality, is what piques a child's appetite. Try transforming a hard-boiled egg into a penguin with the addition of some black olive or raisin eyes, a carrot-tip nose, and toast cutout feet. How about mixing M&M's or raisins inside a scoop of ice cream? I used to hide love notes under a napkin or tie a balloon to the back of a chair. Tiny birthday candles can have a big impact when you put a lit one in a mound of spinach or a baked tomato. When making chocolate chip cookies, it is just as easy to create eyes, a nose, and a smile with the chocolate bits—so, mothers say—why not? As we're amusing ourselves, we're keeping the home fires burning brightly, cheerfully enjoying the process. Our family has grown hopelessly sentimental because of these little, but meaningful, tokens of affection.

The sight of you is good for sore eyes.

— Jonathan Swift

Mothers soften their children with kisses and imperfect noises, with the pap and breast-milk of soft endearments—

— Jeremy Taylor

I loved bringing Alexandra and Brooke into the kitchen to cook with me. One of the saddest realities of contemporary family life is the sense of haste about everything. When mealtime is rushed, mothers rob themselves and their children of savoring all the delicious smells, enjoying decorating cupcakes and cookies, or tearing up lettuce for a salad. Whether we snap green beans or husk corn, peel carrots or make gingerbread cookies, we're doing it together and we are fully engaged. Our energy builds and so does our joy.

During a scary thunderstorm, have an indoor picnic. We used to spread a bistro tablecloth or old worn-out quilt on the kitchen or dining room floor and create a colorful feast. Everyone loves the idea of making their own cream cheese and grape jelly sandwich for a picnic. Keep a stash of large, colorful paper plates for these spontaneous celebrations. Individual packs of potato chips and pretzels are more fun than a bowl full of them. The spirit of an impromptu indoor picnic can turn a frightening storm into a fun event.

Because I was a working mother, I always engaged the girls in cooking with me—I wanted to be with them whenever humanly possible. It made what could have been a routine chore a lot of fun. We've cooked together for so long that it's natural for us to whip up a banquet quickly and smoothly now. There's a special rhythm to it. We each have our favorite tasks and divide up the parts that make the whole so wonderful. The menus continue to change over the years. When Alexandra and

I was never allowed to read the popular American children's books of my day because, as my mother said, the children spoke bad English without the author's knowing it.

— Edith Wharton

Brooke cooked with me as little girls, we'd never heard of salsa or balsamic vinegar, but we'd always enjoy picking up on new recipe ideas.

There are tones of voice that mean more than words.

— Robert Frost

There are some family favorites that I'm always delighted to make whenever they're requested. I learned how to roast the most succulent leg of lamb when I read Julia Child's *Mastering the Art of French Cooking* in 1961. Her recipe is so easy, even a child can follow it. When the girls were old enough to hold a spoon, they helped me with the preparations. They mixed Grey Poupon Dijon mustard with Medaglia d'Oro instant espresso to make a paste. Rather than spoon on this paste, which would have been fun but not memorable, I let them pretend it was finger paint and they slathered it all over the roast, loving the smell. I studded the roast with garlic cloves and the girls put tooth picks where the cloves were so we could pluck them out after the lamb was roasted. The girls loved pouring the entire jar of Spanish olives into the bottom of the roasting pan.

Loving a child doesn't mean giving in to all his whims; to love him is to bring out the best in him, to teach him to love what is difficult.

— Nadia Boulanger

When the lamb is seared at high heat, the juice stays locked inside and the outside becomes blackened. The perfume in the kitchen is award-winning, so we keep the kitchen door flung wide open to allow the anticipation of our leg of lamb to waft into the living room to awaken Peter and gathered family.

I'd let the girls concoct whatever they chose to put on top of the broiled tomatoes. I put bowls and a plate of cheese on the table, so they could combine different ingredients. After careful instruction and a few tiny cuts, they mastered the art of the carrot peeler, which was a great help because they could really zoom through the carrots and potatoes with that gadget. Our joy in sitting together at the kitchen farm table, peeling away, has never left us. We make the same recipe today—the only difference being that the girls now use a spatula to spread the goo on the lamb, and I let them use knives.

I'll never forget the feast many years ago when we let five-year-old Brooke clear the table. Whatever her older sister did, she wanted to do, too. We resisted the obvious instruction of "Don't spill" but we forgot to tell her that the sterling silver knives, forks, and spoons don't get scraped into the garbage along with the food left on the plate. We retrieved our flatware and never said a word. After all, when you're five, sterling silver is no more valuable than a popsicle stick!

> *Two o'clock in the morning courage: I mean unprepared courage.*
>
> — *Napoleon*

Family Rituals

When my girls were young, there were certain ceremonies we engaged in every day. We always ate breakfast and dinner together during the school week. We sat down and took time to have a conversation as well as begin the day with a proper breakfast. My parents insisted on this when I was growing up, and I'm surprised how few families eat breakfast together today. It's lovely to spend the first moments of the day together before we each go our separate ways. Dinner was the pleasant break, when we'd sit down to an attractively served candlelight

...to be a well of affection, and not a fountain; to show children that we love them, not when we feel like it, but when they need it.

— Nan Fairbrother

meal. Candles take only seconds to light, and they have a soothing effect on the soul. All the accumulated struggles of the day seem to fade when a beautiful meal is before us. We often ate in the kitchen. We'd turn off all the overhead lights and leave on only the soft lights under the cabinets. We'd then light candles which turned the kitchen into an enchanting dining room instantaneously.

We'd take turns setting a pretty table. I store my linen napkins in an antique Italian chest of drawers I bought in Florence in 1963. The patina of the fruit wood, covered with authentic worm holes, is so charming, I always smile when I tuck a stack of freshly ironed cotton and linen napkins in the drawers. When we use all these pretty things on an ordinary Tuesday night, we feel special as a family.

From the time the girls were born, I never went shopping alone. As a result, they helped select the dishes, napkins, candles, and glasses we used. What mother wouldn't want her children to love the colors and patterns we see together each day? Whether we went to a thrift shop on Third Avenue in New York and the girls spotted a blue Ming vase for eight dollars, the perfect color for our Connecticut cottage kitchen, or we traveled to an antique show and they discovered a child's Windsor chair, together we selected the beautiful things that surrounded us, adding meaning and memories.

One of our blessed daily rituals was to share a sweet moment together, after teeth were brushed, to say prayers, and tell or read a bedtime story. Then we'd kiss and hug goodnight.

Only a mother knows the full meaning of tucking an angel into bed, turning out the lights, and tiptoeing out of the bedroom. You feel as though you are walking on a cloud that you don't want to disturb. Each time I closed the door to their bedrooms, I emerged reborn. What more miracle do we need than to be a mother entrusted with the nurturing of a young soul?

We still kiss, hug, and tell each other "I love you," transcending time, space, lifting up our spirits to the heavens. I've made a lot of mistakes in my life and will likely continue to do so in the future, but one thing I got right has been spending time with my girls. I was insatiable and I still am.

Being a mother fills our soul with the gift of the transcendent. We're given an inflow of spiritual energy because our soul is attached so solidly to the soul of our child. William James assures us, "There is actually and literally more life in our total soul than we are at any time aware of." A mother is a caregiver, a love giver, tenderly nurturing this precious soul of her child. The family rituals we share weave a spiritual net that supports our children. It gives them faith, hope, and love of life.

> *...a child must know that he is loved for himself, even if he fails or does not compete at all.*
>
> *— Norman M. Lobsenz*

Choosing Priorities

We are capable of doing many things at once for our children. Looking back, it isn't the tidy room or the ironed clothes or the gourmet meals that matter, but the love and attention, the

*...children still
live in their own
world, with its
own set of values
...they deserve
to be listened to
on their terms,
not ours. For
the sake of the
children.*

*— The New
York Times*

"What Grown-ups
Don't Understand"

smiles and the laughter, all the times we shared together that remain the foundation of our children's happiness. But in order to have the time and emotional presence to give our higher self to our children, we have to be able to choose what is most important, at the time, under the circumstances.

When we fail to choose priorities, when we give everything equal importance, we become imbalanced. When we equate having dinner with our children with paying the bills, or reading *Winnie-the-Pooh* with folding the laundry, it's time to readjust our priorities. When we give these things equal time, everything comes at us with equal weight and full force, and we snap.

I had one such episode that still causes me pain whenever I recall it. One evening as I was preparing dinner, I suddenly heard a loud noise; it sounded like an explosion. I could see both girls, so I knew no one had fallen down. I rushed around the counter to see what had happened. There, on the Mexican tile floor, were the remains of a white owl pepper shaker. I adored this little porcelain object. It was not even valuable, but I had bought the set many years ago, before Brooke was born, and had become very attached to it. When I saw it there I just went ballistic. "Brooke," I reprimanded, "how could you have done this? You know how much I love it! It's ruined. You know this is not a toy to play with. I'm so upset I don't know what to do."

I knew Brooke hadn't dropped the owl on purpose, but I lost my temper, nevertheless. And she was shaking all night because of my explosion. Today, we laugh whenever we recall that disaster, but still that moment is nonetheless engraved in stone in my memory and hers.

My friend Claire tells me she feels so awful when she overreacts to her kids: "I know my children will end up on a psychiatrist's couch years from now telling the doctor all the terrible things I said and did!"

Keeping our priorities straight, weighing what is of substance, such as listening to each other, with what is of less importance, such as being right, gives us the space we need to make good choices. *Being* with our child always takes precedence over taking care of errands and chores. Stop vacuuming when a child walks through the door; leave dishes in the sink when you sense an honest communication is timely and you need to look at each other directly, without distraction. Find a cozy spot to sit and connect. The time you spend truly listening to your child will be far more important over a lifetime than immaculate rooms and made beds. Some of the greatest talks I've had with Alexandra and Brooke have been spontaneous. We begin doing simple things together — we arrange flowers, cook, or address envelopes — and then we put our projects behind us or aside, depending on the timing, and seize that immediate experience fully. The tidy room will be messed up, the bed will get jumped on, but the communion between a mother and her child is sacred and eternal.

One of the most important qualities of mothering is consistency. When we do keep our pri-

> *A child is fed with milk and praise.*
>
> — *Charles Lamb*

> *There is more pleasure in loving, than in being loved.*
>
> — *Thomas Fuller*

> The strongest of all warriors are these two—Time and Patience.
>
> — Leo Tolstoy

orities straight our responses become more consistent and we don't suddenly find ourselves flying off the handle at unpredictable times. Consistency gives a child a sense that there is an underlying order in her life so that when events feel overwhelming she knows she has that comforting, reliable place to return to. Knowing what is important to us helps teach our child how to set priorities, too.

Instilling Values

In New York City today, it is rare to walk even a few blocks without passing a homeless person. Your child sees at an early age that there is something terribly wrong when people resort to living on the street, begging for money. I always discussed this problem with Alexandra and Brooke, instead of simply trying to ignore it. I told them these were sad,

> Words of comfort, skillfully administered, are the oldest therapy known to man.
>
> — Louis Nizer

not bad, people who don't always know what to do for themselves. Children have an amazing capacity to understand and to sympathize. I'll never forget when Alexandra came to me at the age of six, asking if we could adopt a child from Asia. When I asked her what had given her the idea, she told me she had seen something on television about poor starving children and

wanted to help. I was so touched by her compassion for a child she didn't even know. We agreed that we'd work together to save money to send to the little girl in Asia. When Brooke heard about the new project she wanted to join in immediately.

When we strip our cupboards bare to take canned goods to church or to the temple or neighborhood school for those less fortunate, we feel the true meaning of the gifts we receive through giving. When we make a batch of corn chowder, we make extra so we can share some with an elderly friend or someone who is sick.

Children are sponges for information and they're eager to imitate us. Being real, being ourselves, teaches children so much more about having good values than any robotic instruction on correct manners. Just as adults do, children absorb the goodness in the people around them. When the girls were young they watched as we all put money in the collection plate at church. One Sunday, Alexandra put in a penny with a note that read, "God, this is all the money I have. Love, Alexandra." The Saint James Church used her note for a stewardship campaign.

You may have tangible wealth untold;/Caskets of jewels and coffers of gold./Richer than I you can never be—/I had a Mother who read to me.

— Strickland Gillilan

Children also listen closely to everything we say. If our children overhear us speaking intolerantly of others—particularly of people who are different from us—how can we expect them to accept others? If you're a snob, chances are you will nurture snobbery in your child. Our thoughtful behavior, our kindness to others, is absorbed in our children's character. So too, can our children affect our own character. Their world is so different from the one we knew at their age that sometimes, our children help *us* to become more open toward others and our changing society.

Mothers can teach almost anything, including safe behavior,

with positive affirmations. Instead of commanding children, "Do not walk out into the street before looking both ways," we can simply and more clearly encourage them to look both ways. Also, complimenting our child when she is conscientious is a better way of reinforcing her good behavior than always pointing out what she is failing to do. We don't have to overteach, robbing our children of initiative, but instead, we can encourage them when they do well. That is how they reach their potential.

Many mothers have a problem when their children discover the power of language through using swear words or silly insults. Often, children who do this succeed in getting a rise out of their parents. My mother once washed my mouth out with soap when I said something vulgar. The best way to teach the power of *good* words is through our own fertile vocabulary and by encouraging our children to learn the thrill and power of discovering new ways of expressing themselves. I'm sure my daughters swore when they were with their friends, but we didn't hear them—I believe largely because they never hear us swear.

> *Put all your eggs in the one basket and—WATCH THAT BASKET.*
>
> — *Mark Twain*

Remember, we're all extremely imitative. When I am in the South for more than a couple of days, I tend to pick up a southern accent. Rather than simply punishing children for saying bad words and crude expressions, parents should offer alternatives. Peter always asked the girls to repeat a new word that they had just learned. Often when they were young he'd mispronounce a big word just to shock them into paying attention. Their ears became attuned to language, alert to every verbal "trap" Peter set. We used to look words up in the dictionary for mental nourishment, and to impress Peter after dinner.

I remember one sweet scene I recently saw in the park. A child tripped and scraped his knee. He sobbed inconsolably as his mother held him in her arms, trying to comfort him. Out of the corner of my eye I noticed a little girl, no more than three years old, clutching her mother's coat with one hand and a lollipop with the other, approach the distraught boy and offer him the candy. The gesture was probably the mother's idea, but undoubtedly it made an impression on both children. What a wonderful way to foster compassion in your children. Rather than discussing sharing, we extend ourselves to others, living our truth, illustrating hundreds of simple ways to exemplify the kind of behavior that makes us kind.

Saying No

It's a child's job to challenge authority, and it's a parent's job to maintain it. This is how we teach them right from wrong. A child may not want to finish her homework before watching her favorite television show and may refuse to eat dinner as a form of protest. As she gets older, she may insist on going to a movie with friends on a school night, or miss family meals while talking on the phone. Threatening her with, "Wait until you have your *own* children," will not get you very far in getting through to her. But setting limits and standing by them will. Limits are the earth under a child's feet, a wall against which they can feel the contours of themselves. Establishing limits will help them now and will give them a secure atmosphere of

Ah, lucky girls who grew up in the shelter of a mother's love— a mother who knows how to contrive opportunities without conceding favors, how to take advantage of propinquity without allowing appetite to be dulled by habit.

— Edith Wharton

You have to stand for something or you'll fall for anything.

— Linda J. Henderson's mother's advice

order and consistency and a framework for the future.

There will always be exceptions to the "house rules," so you do need to keep a measure of flexibility. After Brooke's best friend Courtney died, she broke curfew by what seemed like an eternity. I sat up in the living room for hours, checking the front door every few minutes, wondering why the kitchen phone didn't ring. I tried to stay calm but my mind was racing with worry. When Brooke finally arrived safely home, she sat on the sofa and hugged her sobbing, distraught mother. She explained that she had been with friends, talking about Courtney, and had lost track of the time. My instinct was to let her know adamantly how terrified I had been that something had happened to her, but my conscience made me realize that this was not a time to reestablish rules. I knew I had to be flexible for Brooke's sake. It was not like Brooke not

Go right on and listen as thou goest.

— Dante

to call to ask me if she could stay out late. I saw how deeply she was living her friend's tragic death and I understood how she had lost her balance, in the grief she was sharing with friends.

I'm reminded of the wise words of a noble woman, Helen Keller: "The marvelous richness of human experience would lose something of rewarding joy if there were no limitations to overcome. The hilltop hour would not be half so wonderful if there were no dark valleys to traverse."

When our children are very young, we develop a definite "take charge" attitude because we have to. But as they get older, we must adjust to their growing personalities, opinions, and aspirations which are separate from our own. We must resist confronting them on every decision they make, choosing our issues of disagreement mindfully. Children must be allowed to take chances. This is ultimately how they grow up. When we allow and encourage our children to take action, even when faced with uncertainty—which means making mistakes—we know they can learn to take care of themselves.

You never really understand a person until you consider things from his point of view.

— Harper Lee

Many children confide in me that they're afraid to tell their mothers the truth, fearing their disappointment and harsh punishment. When you're a mother, it is important to be approachable always, never to create an atmosphere in which your child is afraid to tell you the truth.

One of my young friends got "double grounded" by her mother because she took her new red bicycle out in the hall of her apartment building for a little ride. Jennifer fell, damaging her bike and spraining her ankle. She hesitated for over an hour, in severe pain, before confessing the accident to her mother because she knew her mother would be furious. And when she finally told her mother what had happened, sobbing and apologizing profusely, her mother immediately took the bike away and sent her to her room. Jennifer had been told not to ride her bike in the hall, but temptation got the best of her, as it does to all of us at times. I'm not saying Jennifer should have been rewarded for her mischief, but at times like these, a loving caress and kisses from a mother are much more in order than punishment.

Children need love, especially when they do not deserve it.

— Harold S. Hulbert

Why is it that the first word out of so many babies' mouths

is *no*? A mother learns the "art of no" primarily to provide safety for her child as well as for keeping a lid on the development of self-indulgent, bad habits that will be difficult to change once a child becomes older. But when a mother is unable to express a positive attitude in most situations, the child is being deprived of exploring all the possibilities that will allow a full blossoming of her potential. What should saying no provide for a child?

On a family vacation, Brooke and Alexandra presented Peter with a list of eighty-nine reasons why they should have a dog. They were so darling and enthusiastic, persuasive and dear, that Peter was torn between yes and no. As a family, we move around too much and this wouldn't be fair to the dog. Peter had previously cared for three hairy friends: Gilbert, a boxer; La Fayette, a black French poodle; and Hindenberg, a dachshund. He enjoyed the company of these pets, Gilbert especially, but he knew the amount of care they deserved was more than our full lifestyle could handle. So, despite Alexandra and Brooke's aggressive, heartfelt pleas, the answer was *no*. End of conversation.

There is only one happiness in life, to love and be loved.

— George Sand

No is undoubtedly a very important parenting issue. We all wonder how mothers before us dealt with it. Alexandra and Brooke were miserable when they didn't get their way, but Peter and I had to stand by our decisions. Saying *no* teaches children about limits. There are, however, many times when you're caught off guard with an idea spontaneously proposed by a child, leaving you stranded in indecision, which often results in a reflexive *"No!"*

Mothers must learn to say no, but they must also learn not to say no foolishly. The art of saying no takes time to develop. A great many of your child's requests will be reasonable and wonderful. Saying yes to some of them tells her that her impulses are OK and her ideas are valid. She learns to have aspirations and reach for goals. As Pearl S. Buck, author of *The Good Earth,* wrote in referring to the hardships of peasant family life in China: "The young do not know enough to be prudent, and therefore they attempt the impossible—and achieve it, generation after generation."

When Peter was in the army, he was told to always find something positive to tell a soldier before informing the soldier of what he had done wrong. A football coach doesn't tell his starting running back, "Don't fumble." Rather, he says, "Protect the ball." "Make this" is more common and effective than "Don't miss." My experience assures me it is far more effective to tell a client what you like about her room than hurt her feelings by pointing out an eyesore. Peter's career as a trial lawyer taught him to tell his clients what they could say in court, not what they could *not* say. This insight applies to your children as well. Mothers can make their points in a positive way: "You can play basketball until dark, but in the driveway." If curfew is ten o'clock, a mother can kindly say, "Sure you can go to a movie tonight, but be home by ten." When our granddaughter Julia (the daughter of Peter's daughter, Blair) told her parents she wanted them to lease a pony next summer, her father smiled and said, "Julia, what a great idea. We'd all love to have a pony at the Stone House for the summer. Let's start a pony fund. Here's five dollars." Seeing her complete elation, I hired Julia to coordinate some of my clothes for the television show I host, *Homes Across America.* She lined up shoes, slacks, blouses, scarves, and, as a result of her artistic genius, they were all expert matches, won-

> *O mother, mother, make my bed,/O make it soft and narrow.*
>
> — *"Barbara Allen's Cruelty"*

derfully thought through. I paid her twenty dollars, and granted her the title of intern of Alexandra Stoddard, Incorporated, at age nine the youngest one ever. She is a rising star.

When I was five, I went to my mother with the big idea of starting my own garden club, with me as president, of course. She said yes. Mothers, understand how important it is when we say *yes* to our children. The mother's art of *no* is the foundation that grounds and balances our children, so that we can say yes when it's time to do so.

Being a Positive Force

As a mother, you have an amazing opportunity to take possession of and channel all that you know and are still learning about life. Everything is new to a child. You teach your child not only about the great wonders of the world, but about how to live well in a challenging world. You guide your child through the many mysteries of life. Not only do you instill values in your child, but you are his inspiration to live by those values. As a mother, you have tremendous power.

It is the nature of babies to be in bliss.

— Dr. Deepak Chopra

A mother's laughter, her smiles, her love pats, her bear hugs, her reverence for the soul of a child, her pure joy in living—all reach deep, deep into the spirit of her child. When a mother says, "I am the luckiest mother alive because I have you as my daughter"; "You make me *so* happy. You are an angel. I love you, darling"; "You are so wise. I look up to you"; "Your kindness is a great source of strength to me"—she strikes a deep and resonant chord in her child.

Last year, Peter and I spent a weekend in New Jersey with our friends Cathy, Bill, and their ten-year-old-son Christopher. I've known Chris since he was in diapers, and because I see him regularly, we've come to be close friends. Sitting at their sun-drenched kitchen table on that Saturday morning, I asked Chris what he loved most about his mother.

"She loves animals," Chris began. "She's very nice. She's not mean. She's always making me happy. She's funny and charming and stuff."

"Why does she always make you happy?" I asked.

"Because she likes to cook and play tennis. She likes flowers, houses, painters, and friends. She gives in to me more than my dad. She lets me stay up late. Mom is soft. She loves nature, games—card games and Ping-Pong. She's a good sport. Mom taught me that reading is fun. She told me that learning makes you a better person and that creativity is a wonderful thing—I love to draw.

"I got my love of music from my mom. She loves the songs of Jimmy Buffet. Her favorite song is "You Are the Sunshine of My Life" by Stevie Wonder. She even likes the TV show *Chicago Hope*.

"Mom exposed me to art. Her favorite artists are Edouard Manet, Claude Monet, Botticelli, Frank W. Benson, Mary Cassatt, and Roger Mühl.

"Her favorite places are the California vineyards, St. Barts, St. Martin, and Paris. Her favorite color is green, jungle green. She likes blue, pink, white, yellow, and chartreuse. Her

> *The little world of childhood with its familiar surroundings is a model of the greater world. The more intensively the family has stamped its character upon the child, the more it will tend to feel and see its earlier miniature world again in the bigger world of adult life.*
>
> — *Carl Jung*

favorite flower is the gardenia. She likes to get flowers for her birthday, particularly peonies. She likes yellow daffodils, and snapdragons, and peace roses—they are white with pink bands and yellow centers. She likes pale pink, yellow, and white roses. And cosmos.

"Mom's favorite foods are smoked salmon, caviar, pâté, pasta, cheeseburgers, turkey, and fish."

How's that for inspiration! Imagine knowing that you have filled your child's life to the brim like this. Imagine yourself as the vehicle for such pleasure and understanding of all life has to offer.

Cathy is a typical mom and she's completely and utterly crazy about Chris. As you can see by his words, the feeling is mutual.

I was awed by Christopher's knowledge of his mother's pleasures. How many ten-year-old boys know what a peace rose is or who the artists Frank W. Benson and Mary Cassatt are? Chris's precocious intellect could only have come from the thousands of hours he spent with this mother, who includes him in almost everything she does. She has built a solid foundation that will help Chris develop tools to be independent and learn what in the world is beautiful to him.

Children are naturally curious. And that natural curiosity can lead both of you into positive experiences. By joining our children in their explorations and encouraging their adventures, we can enjoy the rewards of discovery right along with them.

My daughters loved going to visit my father, who had retired on the west coast of Florida. Our daily mission was to collect seashells, something we've done together since the girls could crawl. If a beach was rocky, we'd collect stones and sea glass. We've brought sand home in glass jars and collected smooth stones, adding them to our treasured collection of sea shells. The scallop shell is our favorite. (When we selected blue stationery for our cottage, we had the engraver put a white scallop shell at top center; a happy symbol for us, intensified because it is the logo of St. James Church in New York City where our dear friend John Bowen Coburn married Peter and me.)

The conclusion is always the same: love is the most powerful and still the most unknown energy of the world.

— Pierre Teilhard de Chardin

All our years of beachcombing enhanced our curiosity about underwater life. We love to go snorkeling together and point out nature's glories to one another. When the girls were young, we used to look up in a sea life encyclopedia all the colorful fish we had spotted on our water adventure. Then we'd visit the Museum of Natural History to get more information on the ocean environment. Sometimes the girls still surprise me with the knowledge they've retained.

We came to call these luscious periods "grooves," when we were in no danger of being brought down by schedules and time. When I eat scallops, I'm always reminded of their pretty fan-shaped shells and the beach grooves I enjoyed with my daughters. As a family, we are always drawn to the seashore where we play, swim, and never tire of our seashell collecting — all souvenirs of beaches we've loved.

I've been so lucky to travel together with my daughters.

We've watched perfume being made in Grasse, France, been to department stores and pharmacies all over the world, enjoying the sprays and the goos, the scents, and the sensational packaging. Whenever we travel to Europe, we take few toiletry items with us so we can stock up on deodorant, colorful cotton balls, and colored emery boards. One French perfume is bottled in a frosted glass cone with a ball finial on top, a work of art with a magic potion inside. This is a girls' thing, a groove we shall never subject Peter to; we meet him at an outdoor café after we've stocked up.

Curiosity leads us up every escalator, to comb all floors. Who knows if there's a bargain to be found? We've bought striped face mitts for luxuriating in the bath and plaid patterned boxes, flower clippers, place mats, trays, and napkins. Because of my passion for stationery supplies, the girls come with me to stock up on my colored Bristol cards, file folders, pens, ink cartridges, clipboards, binders, and scissors. For themselves, they might find a pen holder, some botanical-garden wrapping paper, or the wired French ribbon that they love. Interior decorators instinctively cast about, looking for something unusual, something practical that is well made and imaginatively designed.

> *I have yet to see anyone who did not respond to tenderness in action.*
>
> — *Eknath Easwaran*

Now that my daughters have their own apartments, I look back on our whirlwind trips throughout department stores, moving in all directions, and wonder if perhaps these experiences helped train their eyes and develop their sense of style. When Brooke moved into her own apartment, I helped her paint her bathroom lilac, above white tile walls up to the wainscoting. The bathroom has a

black-and-white mosaic tile floor, white fix-
tures, and chrome hardware.

I always loved to take Alexandra and
Brooke to Paley Park, a vest-pocket park on
Fifty-third Street between Madison and Fifth
Avenues. We'd always sit close to the spray of
the waterfall wall, sip a soda, and simply appreciate the scene. We discovered dozens of places
of natural beauty in New York where we
always found comfort and joy. In the spring
we'd sit on the marble wall at the Four Seasons
Restaurant, warmed by the sun, surveying the
majestic reflecting pools and fountains. The
garden at the Museum of Modern Art was
another special place, combining natural beauty
with the powerful energy of sculpture.
Museums were, and continue to be, inspiring
places where my daughters and I love to be
together. We go to be amused, entertained, and
above all stimulated, each of us leaving with our
creativity refreshed and with a clearer vision of
ways to express ourselves.

A friend who has two sons spends a lot of
time learning about every creature and natural
phenomenon from dinosaurs to cocoons,
watching the Discovery Channel as well as
reading books. Our children find an inchworm fascinating, a
seashell inspiring, a lady bug adorable, and a bird's nest sweet.
As children, Thomas Edison, Albert Einstein, Albert
Schweitzer, Rachel Carson, Amelia Earhart, and Ralph Waldo
Emerson must have been challenges to parents trying to keep

...the first step toward becoming a solid parental unit is for the man and woman to develop a strong mutual attraction. The genetic payoff of having two parents devoted to a child's welfare is the reason man and woman can fall into swoons over one another, including swoons of great duration.

— Robert Wright

a few steps ahead of their young, curious geniuses and visionaries.

Perhaps one of the most wondrous, juicy, happy examples we can set for our children is when we relax. My mother was so conscientious that I actually found it relaxing to see her just sitting in a chair, calmly taking pleasure in the moment. Mother was a voracious reader, so there were always books nearby. She read for enrichment and for pleasure. You could see a visible lift in her mood whenever she had a book in hand.

> *To be uncertain is to be uncomfortable, but to be certain is to be ridiculous.*
>
> — *Chinese proverb*

I also remember being thrilled whenever my parents dressed up to go out for the evening to have fun with friends or whenever my mother took a bubble bath. Children watch their parents to learn about life. Every pleasure we take, each thing we enjoy, shows them the delights that await them in their own lives.

However, though it pains us, we cannot always protect our children from the darkness and sadness in the world. That is finally up to fate, luck, and circumstance. Although there is pain and misfortune, we can provide our children with the encouraging truth that within every cloud there is indeed a silver lining—even though it is sometimes barely detectable. Our children will experience pain and danger; they will feel disturbed and confused by seeing homeless people while on their way to school; they will be bewildered by the death of a loved one; and they will feel gravely disappointed by rejections from lovers, friends, and the outside world. But if

> *...enthusiasm is the source of creativity.*
>
> — *Dr. René Dubos*

we succeed in teaching them that although problems will arise, every problem holds within it the seed to its solution, they will grow up bolstered by their knowledge that they are strong enough to face anything that may come.

When I was growing up, our cocker spaniel Chumily was run over by a car and killed. Ever since I was eleven and lost my favorite pet dog, I've realized how universal pain is. It doesn't matter how old we are; we all suffer. My sister and I had two cats, Adrian and Boutique, at our farm in upstate New York. They lived in the hay loft in the horse barn. One morning, I approached the barn, calling, "Here Adrian, here, Boutique. Here, here, pussycats." The dew had lifted and the sun was warm. The day was full of promise. As I climbed the ladder to the loft, I kept calling for Adrian and Boutique. My horse, Comanche Chief, whinnied and I remember hearing the rustle of hay under my bare feet. I saw blood, and, horrified, I spotted the remains of their ravished bodies. They'd been killed and half-eaten by wild animals.

Mother's love grows by giving.

— Charles Lamb

My mother was wonderful. She understood how much we loved our dog and cats who had died so suddenly when we were at tender ages. Both times, she gave our pets a funeral. We chose a sacred place where they were honored, helping us heal and keep the loving memories alive.

Months before I knew my brother Powell was having open-heart surgery, Brooke, Peter, and I had planned a trip to Paris in early February. Powell died during surgery at the end of January. His sudden death moved us to keep our plans and make our trip to France a celebration of life. We persuaded Alexandra to take time off from work to join us. Our journey allowed us to grieve together and cheer up one another as only we could do as a family. We grow spiritually when we endure pain and sadness. These are the transition times when we deepen our compassion and appreciation of life. We're moved into a wider perspective. Being together in one of our favorite places, treasuring each moment, seizing every opportunity to live vitally, helped each of us to accept our loss and comforted the girls that they needn't worry about me. When we're together, we're strong and we carry that strength with us when we're separated.

To forbid us anything is to make us have a mind for it.

— Michel de Montaigne

By emphasizing what is true, what is ennobling, what is beautiful, we remind our children about something basic to existence: that comfort and/or joy are always possible, even in our darkest hour. Experiencing nature, being with friends, and enjoying art can always lift me out of myself and provide an opportunity to make a divine connection. But being with my daughters when I am hurting or when they are in pain is always transforming.

What are the greatest gifts you can give your child? You can care for your child, sacrifice, educate, feed, clothe, shelter, teach morals, and teach virtue by example. But above all these, I believe, the greatest legacy you can ultimately give your child is your pure, loving, warm heart, and your love of life.

Being There

If I had to begin my life as a mother again, I'd make a more conscientious effort not to be in a hurry. As an interior designer, I go into many people's homes and I see that many mothers are too busy, in too much of a rush, to spend time with their children. And that troubles me. In some cases, it is unavoidable. Your son's soccer practice runs late so you can't be on time to pick your daughter up from school. You have to stay late at work so you don't have time to build that dollhouse you promised to build for your daughter tonight. There is an endless list of things you have to do that prevent you from spending important times with your child. But in order to really *be there* for your children, you have to put many things aside.

When our child is in need, we instinctively want to drop everything, for our world is now this one person who needs us. I've canceled business trips minutes before going to the airport. I've postponed important meetings when Alexandra and Brooke needed me at their side—for whatever reason. I never resented being there for my children, nor did I consider it a sacrifice. I never felt that I was forfeiting anything, because my children only added to my life. Admittedly, I was exhausted at times, but that didn't change the fact that I loved every minute that I shared with my daughters. They were the best company anyone could wish for. Looking back, the greatest blessing was *being there,* hanging around when there were no special needs, and when there were, dropping everything to do whatever I could. Ultimately, being there, as a loving presence, was the gift we gave to one another.

There were times when the demands of being mother, busi-

> *There are innumerable people who have a wide choice between saving and giving their children the best possible opportunities. The decision is usually in favor of the children.*
>
> — *Eleanor Roosevelt*

nesswoman, wife, and homemaker "whelmed" me. My friend and first editor, Kate Medina, corrected me once when I confided to her that I felt overwhelmed when Alexandra was in the hospital with pneumonia, Brooke was home with bronchitis, and I was exhausted from the stress. Kate smiled, and told me, "Alexandra, you have a big life. Right now, there's a lot going on. But you're strong. You may be 'whelmed' but you're not *over*whelmed." And she was right. When you put your children first, above the appearance of your home, before your career or social life or personal interests, you find the bond between you is more sacred. No one seeking an easy life becomes a mother. Mothers are stretched, challenged, and, at times, extremely tired. But everything works out once you commit yourself to being there for your children.

> *Now run along, and don't get into mischief. I am going out.*
>
> *— Beatrix Potter*

One of the most important questions for married women with children today is a practical one: How do we divide the labor at home? Many men will share some of the housework, but primarily, it is still the woman who really has to wear all the hats at once. Peter often tells me he can do only one thing at a time, and I believe him. I've never heard a mother say that. If she did, she wouldn't be telling the truth.

Although most women do manage well and enjoy their ability to feed, clothe, and nurture their children while also doing their own work, at times the weight gets too great. Each mother has her unique coping skills. When she doesn't expect to be supported, she becomes more self-reliant, and usually manages quite well. Whenever a mother turns against her husband, she defeats herself.

Years ago there was a cartoon in *The New Yorker* of a mother holding two babies, with a toddler tugging at her leg. Dressed in a gray pinstriped suit, swinging his brown leather briefcase, newspaper tucked under his arm, Daddy trips over toys, and kisses her good-bye: "Off to the office, dear." To which she replies: "Ralph, it's Sunday."

Sometimes women feel that their husbands aren't there for their children in the same way that they are. To a certain extent, they're right. Fathers are around for the weekend, but generally come and go with greater freedom than mothers. Husbands can avoid everything from changing diapers and getting breakfast ready to taking their child to school or attending birthday parties and school plays. This imbalance doesn't have to cause difficulties, but sometimes it does, when we have idealized expectations based on how things should be, but aren't—at least, not yet. There are no compromises when children are the issue being argued: Parents have to be there for them—even if one parent does more than the other. In the end, the gains we reap from our attentions to children far outweigh the effort it costs us. Many fathers "catch on," as my friend John Coburn suggests, but some never do. Being there is the joy. That's the honey. That's what makes *everything* worthwhile.

Many parents do divide up necessary tasks, but there is rarely a complete switch of roles. When my daughters were growing up, Peter regularly helped out, in his own way, but not in the same way I did. If I was cooking dinner and the girls were playing jacks on the cork floor, Peter would come home from work, sit at the kitchen table, and rather than *do* anything

> *Training a baby by the book is a good idea, only you need a different book for each baby.*
>
> — Dan Bennett

visibly useful or practical, he'd be available to us, interested and interesting, making us feel loved, appreciated, and secure.

Nowadays, the parenting responsibilities between mothers and fathers are beginning to be shared. The goal should not be for fathers to relieve mothers of "child time," but to join in the fun of raising the children as a family. When both parents are present for a child on a daily basis, her sense of security is greater and that enriches her self-confidence.

> *Have a heart that never hardens, and a temper that never fires, and a touch that never hurts.*
>
> *– Charles Dickens*

What's most important here is *how* we are when we're there for our children. What does it mean for a parent to "be there" for a child? Nurturing a child is not exclusively about shared responsibilities; it's about being there. It's not about magically knowing what to do. Efficiency has no place in raising children. If Dad is *there*, then he is the mom. Care has no gender. Being there is the point.

We have come a long way to bring men into the center of parenting, but often we mothers still can't take for granted that our husbands are able and willing to take on maternal responsibilities, to be on call twenty-four hours a day.

Oddly enough, although I often felt frantic, I loved my two years as a single mother. The girls' father had moved to Los Angeles, and the girls and I lived in New York, so there was no denying that I alone was essentially raising them. They visited their father for seven weeks every summer and on a few other selected vacations. I may have slept fewer hours because of this arrangement, but the joy I experienced with Alexandra and Brooke was well worth the exhaustion I felt. I was busy with my girls, enjoying their company and taking care of their needs. It's funny, but it's possible that knowing that I was the only one there to take care of them helped me readily accept full responsibility—without misgivings.

Every marriage is different. When I remarried, Peter and I discussed how we would manage finances and we made tentative plans for how we would live. He told me right away that he had no intention of disciplining the girls, who were seven and four at the time. That was up to me and their father. I accepted that gladly because I'd been accustomed to this role as a single mother. He would be there as a supportive, loving parent, enjoying spending time together, having fun as a family. I depended on Peter for advice, sympathy, encouragement, and companionship. In turn, he helped out regularly, not as an obligation, rather as a bonus.

In villages the world over men spend the daylight hours doing strenuous labor and the women spend ninety hours a week, day *and* night, doing household chores. It isn't likely a woman can grab her husband and get him to help her out after he's completed his work. Mothers have the capacity to be the center of their children's lives throughout their entire childhood. Any help received along the way is a gift. But to beg, badger, and bicker in order to gain a little help here and there deflates the whole energy and atmosphere of joy you establish with your child.

No one likes to be pushed around. When there is a loving energy at home, family members will all want to hang around

We cooked, cleaned, laboured, worried, planned, we wept and laughed, we groaned and we sang—but we never despaired. All this was but a passing phase; "we will certainly laugh at this someday," we all said buoyantly, laughing even then.

— Kathleen Norris

one another more. Fathers will gradually "catch on," offering to help out and do necessary tasks without being asked. The secret is to be so calm and self-contained that your husband will feel drawn into the joyful aura created by you and the children. I'm sure that we can all do more, and be there for our children more than we may know.

> *A merry heart maketh a cheerful countenance.*
>
> — *Proverbs*

The more we are present for our children, the calmer we become. The mother who has not made a genuine commitment to making her children her top priority will feel scattered, frenetically running around feeling anxious and guilty. My artist friend Marysarah Quinn, who designed this book, told me recently, "Alexandra, since Dylan was born everything has changed. Mark and I are Dylan's parents and we put him first. We make no decisions that don't consider what's best for Dylan. It feels so right to be his mom."

Because being a mother rarely allows us to be on the circumference, where we are only partially involved with our children's lives, we have to learn to stay centered emotionally in the midst of all the distractions, for our own sake as well as for the best interests of our children.

Anne Morrow Lindbergh understood all the forces that pull at women, particularly mothers, in her wonderful book *Gift from the Sea: An Answer to the Conflicts in Our Lives:*

> For to be a woman is to have interests and duties, raying out in all directions from the central mother-core, like spokes from the hub of a wheel.
>
> The pattern of our lives is essentially circular. We must be open to all points of the compass; husband, chil-

dren, friends, home, community; stretched out, exposed, sensitive like a spider's web to each breeze that blows, to each call that comes.... How much we need, and how arduous of attainment is that steadiness preached in all rules for holy living.

The key to being *present* for your children, of making sure they are always aware of your love, nurturing, and support, is your sense of delight in them. You need to be *there* during times of calm and celebration as well as in times of crisis. Remember that everything is a big deal to children. *Be there* to congratulate them on a good grade or a still-wet finger painting; *be there* to read them to sleep; *be there* to wipe away the tears when they hurt; *be there* to put eight Band-Aids on that boo-boo when one would do; *be there* to answer questions, whether they are serious or trivial; *be there* to watch them do three somersaults in a row; *be there* so they know they are the most precious part of your life. A mother's divine *presence* is always noticed. When we are absent physically, emotionally, and spiritually, a void is deeply felt by our children. When we are channels of this loving energy, our children will thrive.

Being *present* requires profound concentration on what we're doing as we go along. You can't show up late for an event, a nervous wreck, fidgeting, anxious, your mind somewhere else. Mindfulness requires focusing on what's before you, living inside each moment, absorbing the experience fully, watching, feeling, sensing. When we are present, we are utilizing our higher powers. When we pay attention, we are connected to a higher perspec-

> *I do not love him because he is good but because he is my child.*
>
> *— Rabindranath Tagore*

tive, a deeper, more vital appreciation of what's happening. In this alertness, we are transformed by enthusiasm for our child, for ourself, for life.

Children generally hate to be idle. All the care then should be, that their busy humor should be constantly employed in something that is of use to them.

— John Locke

Mothers always know.

— Oprah Winfrey

Dr. Irwin Chabon, who delivered Brooke, wrote a book entitled *Awake and Aware.* In it he discussed how we can train our minds to focus on one object in order to control the pain. I never had so much as an aspirin giving birth to both my children. By being there, "awake and aware," I was completely tuned into what was happening. I was *there* for this miracle. I would have hated to have been asleep or numb. Thankfully, I had the good fortune of being young, healthy, and fit enough so that natural childbirth was the best option. But I understand that many women cannot have natural childbirth for any number of reasons. I believe that being awake and aware more importantly applies to our state of awareness during our child's growth. We can all do this. Every gift of our *presence* to our child is grace. Life cannot become sweeter than when we are fully present for our children.

What do mothers do for their children? They radiate joy from the happiness they feel in being such important, essential people in their children's lives. Mothers are their children's greatest fans. We brag about them behind their backs; we exaggerate their talents and skills and overlook their shortcomings. While we help our children to blossom into generous adults, the greatest gift we give them is our spirit. All the hard work, the sacrifices, the sleep deprivation, the worrying, are all spokes from this central hub of the wheel.

Recently, I was deeply touched by an essay that appeared in *The New York Times*. It was written by Amelia H. Chamberlain, a high-school student in Queens, New York, who had entered and won a writing contest with the theme "A Woman I Admire." She wrote about her mother:

> I tell her not to push herself, but she says we need the money.... All too quickly she has to leave. She hands me my $3.60 for school and kisses me on the cheek. As always, she tells me she loves me. Then she walks out the door and drives off to her job.
>
> How does she do it? How does she always remember to give me $3.60 for school? How does she always remember to tell me that she loves me? How does she work all night and do errands all day? How does she raise me and my sisters on her own? She never gives up and says, "I can't go today." She never, ever, doesn't get up, no matter how little sleep she's gotten....
>
> I turn my eyes toward God and silently thank the Lord for Mama.

...her smile was like a rainbow after a sudden storm.

— *Colette*

What more is there to say about what mothers do? The list is endless as the love of a mother for her children is infinite.

Chapter 4

Esteeming and Loving Ourselves

The ultimate lesson of life all of us have to learn is unconditional love, which includes not only others but ourselves as well.

—*Elisabeth Kübler-Ross,*
On Death and Dying

To Thine Own Self Be True

As mothers, it is possible for us to become so wrapped up in caring for our children and our families that our own inner growth and balance is jeopardized. Many of us fail to recognize that often our fatigue and frustration around our children occur because we have forgotten to tend to ourselves. We become sullen and edgy, and our short tempers prevents us from enjoying life.

> *Cherish that which is within you.*
>
> *— Chuang-tzu*

My mother was keenly aware that always being on call for others would wear away at her sense of self, and often, she would dramatically recite these, her favorite lines from Shakespeare's *Hamlet,* to remind herself and those around her of the importance of self-respect:

To thine own self be true, and it must follow, as the night
    the day,
Thou canst not then be false to any man.

Today a new sun rises for me; everything lives, everything is animated, everything seems to speak to me of my passion, everything invites me to cherish it.

— Anne de Lenclos

Mother was passionate about those words. Looking back now, I can see that her belief in them had a profound, positive influence on me and on how I raised Alexandra and Brooke. Because Mother was extremely capable of following through on her conviction, especially later in her life when she refused to have her identity tied up in family obligations—she was able to leave enough free time to pursue some of her many interests.

How can we, as mothers, be true to ourselves? How can we continuously find fresh ways to nourish our minds and souls as we concentrate on doing the same for our children? How can we stay flexible, vigorous, and focused as we run after spirited children? How can we expand our consciousness and awaken to new spiritual dimensions? How can we maintain our own identity—keeping it fresh and unique—so it never becomes clouded, as we are absorbed with the lives of others?

I often think of that wonderful expression "space to breathe." Mothers need space to breathe, to replenish their spirits, every day. This space, a place where the self is reawakened, is available to every mother. You only have to set your sights on it to find your reawakened self.

Claiming Time for Yourself

Amid the chaos of mothering, the first way I regained my balance was to take time for myself. Like having a drink after a long thirst, a mother who claims her own time is refreshed and restored to herself. When you are hungry, you need to eat. When you are constantly pulled away from yourself by the demands of children, you need to come back to yourself to feel OK. I've incorporated solitude, even brief moments of it, into my life as a regular practice. Czech-born Franz Kafka, who wrote in German, beautifully described such moments of quiet meditation and the many opportunities we have for experiencing these moments:

This Self is the honey of all beings, and all beings are the honey of this Self.

— Brihadaranyaka Upanishad

> You need not leave your room. Remain sitting at your table and listen. You need not even listen, simply wait. You need not even wait, just learn to become quiet, and still, and solitary. The world will freely offer itself to you to be unmasked. It has no choice; it will roll in ecstasy at your feet.

In China, they must know something about the human need to draw oneself inward during the course of the day. In one small village, a lovely ritual of solitude is performed every single day. At a random time, a bell rings out, at which point everyone, no matter what their age or position in the commu-

> *What is the seal of liberation?— No longer being ashamed in front of oneself!*
>
> — *Friedrich Nietzsche*

nity, stops what he or she is doing and for a few minutes, becomes still.

I have gotten into the habit of creating restorative rituals out of almost everything I do. Doing so elevates a common, everyday experience into something that touches and raises my spirits. When I begin to feel exasperated and overburdened by the demands of others, I try to find the meditative place that Kafka describes. Whether it requires that I stop what I'm doing and meditate or that I integrate this solitude into something I'm already doing, such as something physical, including household chores, I make it a point to find time to be in touch with my own needs.

Sometimes when I need time alone, I scrub my butcher-block counters or polish tabletops in the living room. At those times, when no one disturbs me, I usually play a beautiful piece of music (Beethoven's "Moonlight Sonata" or George Winston's "December"), or spiritual tapes such as recordings of sermons by John Bowen Coburn or Eric Butterworth, to further clear and relax my mind. In those twenty minutes or so I feel reconnected with my heart and soul; I feel an overwhelming sense of comfort and joy. I find that these pleasurable interludes make it easier to face all the activity of family life. I come up refreshed and restored. You can do the same for yourself in your own home. You don't have to go to church or synagogue to pray. When you do things in a deliberate, quiet, meditative way, it is like saying a prayer. In your mind you are communing with a higher force and expressing gratitude for your life.

> *Like a child, your body wants attention and feels comforted when it receives it.*
>
> — *Dr. Deepak Chopra*

At other times, when I need to be still as opposed to doing something physical, I take Zen time. This is my opportunity to sit calmly, in a sacred place, and meditate. If you don't have a sacred place in your home, claim one. The marble tabletop in the living room of our New York apartment is my place. Whenever I need pure calm, I know it is there for me. The marble is always cool, and it soothes my nerves. The table is positioned in front of two large, sunny windows that look out on a church steeple set against the sky. I bought this antique table in France more than thirty years ago, and it simply has good karma. I always place fresh flowers on this table, which adds to the lovely, tranquil atmosphere. I usually light a candle, even in the daytime, and place it on the table as well. Who is to say what time is appropriate to light a candle in your own home? Over the years I guess I've spent several thousand hours here, at this table. I come to it for strength, for a sense of wholeness and for a feeling of transcendence. Here is where I nourish my soul in a way that is unique; what I do here is for me.

> *Life was meant to be lived. Curiosity must be kept alive.... One must never, for whatever reason, turn his back on life.*
>
> *— Eleanor Roosevelt*

Once, when I went to my table to meditate and write, I discovered Peter seated with legal papers spread out over its entire surface. I was shocked to see him seated at my place. Peter quickly realized how truly symbolic this space was to me and the importance of always having it available for my use. This place is my shrine to a calm, composed, undisturbed moment's peace.

You can create a sacred space anywhere in or around your home. Perhaps your space will be in your garden, in a spot where it is private and shaded. Or perhaps the sacred spot can be a worn but well-loved rocker in the kitchen or living room. When you find your sacred space, let every family member know that this is your chair, your corner of the room, your retreat. Soon you will look forward to whatever moments you find to savor your sense of space.

You were once wild here. Don't let them tame you!

— Isadora Duncan

Some mothers, unfortunately, have a hard time acknowledging that they even have a need for separateness, to reconnect with themselves. But why? Surely mothers, like their children, need to be tended to. A mother doesn't get nourishment by watching her children eat. She, too, needs food. Doesn't it then follow that a mother not only gets pleasure from watching her children thrive but also needs to do what she enjoys? This is not impossible to do, no matter what your circumstance. It may not always be easy, and there may be times when you simply cannot take time for yourself, but you *can* do it.

Children Do Not Make Us Complete

When we were single, we may have believed our lives would be complete when we got married. Once we were married, many of us believed our lives would be fulfilled only when we had children. But we have discovered, as we pass each of these milestones, that completeness can only come from within. Feeling complete is something you must recreate and nurture every single day. Completeness does not come when we cross another item off life's "to do" list. We never really stop developing. Our bodies and the circumstances of our lives constantly change, as do our needs. At the same time, our spiritual and intellectual selves continue to develop and deepen. In a sense, our lives are never complete.

No matter how much of our time is consumed with caring for our children, we should always seek out new experiences that will enrich our spirit. We have needs that only *we* can satisfy. We need quiet times to calm the muddy waters in our soul, and to find stillness at the center of a full, vigorous, exciting life. If we can't find grace right here, right now, in the midst of all this activity, do we honestly think it will suddenly appear on its own?

In her autobiography, *Me,* Katharine Hepburn writes that her mother gave her some advice that she undoubtedly took to heart. She told her daughter, "If you always do what interests you, then at least one person will be pleased." Hepburn was married very briefly and never had children, but she certainly learned how to enjoy herself.

As a woman, I am whole only when I'm able to open up my heart to myself and to those I care for. In fact, it was through this self-nurturing that I began to understand the sacredness of being a mother. Taking time out for myself, even if it was just a few minutes, helped me get in touch with the power of my maternal role. In coming back to myself I understood how much care I had to give, how much patience I had to have to navigate the rocky seas of motherhood, and I realized all the more keenly what it was I did for my children; how much mindfulness I had to exercise for them. Respecting my own needs was better for all of us in the end.

> *First keep peace within yourself, then you can also bring peace to others.*
>
> — Thomas à Kempis

> *He that would govern others, first should be/ The master of himself.*
>
> — Philip Massinger

Set a Good Example

To be true to ourselves, we must look into our hearts and make sure we don't say one thing and do another. Not only did my mother often cite those lines quoted earlier from Shakespeare, but she was also able to follow through on the spirit of his words. Doing so not only made her a more ful-filled, more well-rounded person, her content-ment helped me to be a happier, more stable child. Her belief that life is meant to be enjoyed helped set a model for me to follow my own internal dictates. Despite her tendency toward perfectionism, my mother did know how to relax and enjoy life. Watching Mother tend her garden, decorate and enjoy her beautiful home, and go tooling around in her car was not only thrilling to wit-ness, but her pleasure showed me it was OK and good to take joy in one's pleasures.

It's all right for a woman to be, above all, human.

— Anaïs Nin

By being true to herself, a mother sets an important exam-ple for her children to do the same. Fulfilling our individual potential is essential to giving our children our full force; it is a way to be true to them.

The other woman in my life who set an example of how a mother honors herself by tending to her own happiness as well as that of her children was Peter's mother, Miriam. Her life has much to teach all mothers about how to sustain ourselves even as we care for others. I never saw Miriam without a twinkle in her eye. Many mothers feel this same boundless devotion to their children, but not all mothers exude Miriam's sense of joy in all of life. Somehow Miriam always managed to make sure she nurtured and nourished herself. This, I believe, was an essential ingredient to her general happiness.

Miriam made time to paint, read historical novels, swim, run, play backgammon, and sew petit point. She painted folding screens, and if the decorating budget didn't permit expensive wallpaper, Miriam would paint a mural of a historic scene she'd dream up from her history reading. Rather than having ordinary chair seats, she'd petit point the dining room chairs with favorite flowers and plants in all the colors she adored.

> *The greatest part of our happiness or misery depends on our dispositions and not on our circumstances.*
>
> *— Martha Washington*

Miriam also periodically indulged herself. She had her own passions, which had nothing to do with being a mother. She collected semiprecious stones that she would take to a jewelry store on Madison Avenue where they would be set into "gubby" rings and pins. Her husband loved her colorful gems and the children were glad to see how much pleasure these items brought their mother. The purple star sapphire and pale green cabochon emerald rings I always wear were gifts from Grandmother Brown because she felt my ring finger "looked so lonely." Recently, Miriam's daughter, Bebe, my ladies' tennis doubles partner in the 1950s, smiled and said, "Mother would be so happy knowing how much you treasure her rings. I've never seen you without them." Miriam also never shied away from taking to her chaise longue and putting her feet up if she needed a breather from her activities.

> *A cheerful woman is one who has cares but doesn't let them get her down.*
>
> *— Beverly Sills*

Miriam also made a point of maintaining her physical health. Being a mother of four active

Your success and happiness lie in you.... Resolve to keep happy, and your joy and you shall form an invincible host against difficulties.

— Helen Keller

children, she did a lot of bending, stretching, and running around. You have to be fit for whatever work you take on; in her childrearing days Miriam could outrun her kids. She lived in a time before aerobics classes and understood that a housewife who ran up and down the stairs, made beds, and ran errands got plenty of exercise. As a bride she had a nineteen-inch waist. Even after she gave birth to four children, I'm not sure it expanded more than a few inches. Miriam also ate carefully; she believed that eating a little of everything was the best way to maintain a healthful diet: "You never know when some report will come out saying you need a little of this or that in your diet," she often instructed. The meals she prepared for her family were varied and delicious.

Miriam never outgrew her playfulness. With four children to skip around with, she remained agile and spunky. She adored the beach, the sun, and particularly the ocean; she loved to shoot the waves along with her children. She also enjoyed reading on the beach, always wearing a hat and sitting under an umbrella to avoid damaging her skin. Miriam continued to exercise regularly and remained physically active until she moved into a nursing home just before her ninetieth birthday.

I cannot think of any mother who lived a more balanced and whole life than Miriam. She is a model for me for how a mother honors herself by doing all the things she loves. Peter's life and his love for Miriam are luminous tributes to her richness as both a mother and a human being.

A happy, fulfilled mother is a model to her children for so

many reasons. She breaks the mold and does things her own way. Because she remains true to herself, she has the strength to allow her children to experiment with ways of being true to themselves. A mother who is afraid of being her own person will be reluctant to allow her children to take the chances they need to take in order to be themselves. She will hold her children back just as she has held herself back from living fully. A vital, self-nurturing mother gives children the confidence that they, too, will find their own way.

Walk Away from Unfinished Work

But how, you may ask, do we find this copious free time, this luxury to nurture and develop ourselves, to take time out to meditate or to be solitary? One of the things we can all do is take a good, hard look at all the things we do and ask ourselves, do we need to do them all? We mothers can learn to build minibreaks into our schedules to ensure private time, no matter how demanding or hectic life becomes. Back in the 1970s, when I was really struggling to maintain grace under pressure, I wrote a book that was never published called *Taking Time*. I was raising two daughters, working, handling financial obligations, writing, and going from one church service to another on a spiritual quest, soaking up all the different philosophies of life. In short, my life

> *Woman must not accept; she must challenge. She must not be awed by that which has been built up around her; she must reverence that woman in her which struggles for expression.*
>
> *— Margaret Sanger*

was brimming over with activity. Luckily, I had learned from my mother how to claim time for myself. When she was raising four children, somehow she managed to drive forty-five minutes from our house in Westport to New Haven, Connecticut, to study architecture under Vincent Scully at Yale University.

She sneaked out while we were still at school, letting the housekeeper supervise us until she returned in the late afternoon. She always appeared radiant when she returned from those stimulating sessions.

Ring the bells that still can ring/Forget your perfect offering./There is a crack in everything./That's how the light gets in.

— Leonard Cohen

How did she do it? She learned to claim time for herself by walking away from unfinished work. Must we finish cleaning all the dishes before taking time for ourselves? Can't the extra load of laundry wait till tomorrow? Doing what fills our hearts and minds with inspiration is a far higher priority than cleaning the dust off the living room furniture.

Walking away from unfinished work can be difficult, but it can be done. I've found ways of managing household maintenance so that daily life operates relatively smoothly, without any overdoing. I start by having realistic expectations. If I don't complete a chore, I don't let it get to me because I know it's all a never-ending process. I limit the number of loads of laundry I do per week, and I *always* break for a leisurely lunch no matter what I may be in the middle of doing at the time. If the spirit moves me, I take a two-minute bath, maybe even a few times in one day, and as a result, return to my chores refreshed and with added energy.

I began to reset my priorities when I realized that if I finished all the housework every day, to the point of being "caught up," I'd never have any time for myself. I understand the eagerness and the satisfaction of mothers who stretch themselves to the limit, but stretching to the point of wearing out is no solution. Less, in this case, can be more. In the end, we lose more satisfaction than we gain. We have to make a deliberate plan and stick with it until taking time for ourselves becomes a habit. Set your alarm a little earlier for a quiet, private half hour or so to yourself before you start your day. Eventually, your body will automatically wake itself up without any alarm. Or make a plan to go to a movie by yourself or with a friend once a month. As the Greek philosopher Aristotle taught us, "We are what we repeatedly do."

> *Set aside the moments for activities that will help you to center and find emotional tranquility.*
>
> *— Greta K. Nagel*

Another strategy for cutting back on your work schedule is learning how to let others do things for you. I was efficient, as was my mother before me. If something needed to be fixed, I was there to do it. But I've learned I don't have to do everything just because I can. I've learned to let Peter do more and more. Peter writes most of the thank-you notes, buys gifts from the two of us, and helps me keep the apartment filled with flowers, which he arranges. Many mornings he brings me breakfast in bed, and he always handles travel arrangements with our travel agent. More often than I do, he takes care of firewood, cleaning supplies, and even groceries.

Every mother has to figure out for herself how to find this time. You can hire a baby-sitter so you can go to the library to read or do research, just take a walk, or do some fun shopping on your own. There are many creative ways to find quiet time without incurring exorbitant costs. If you don't feel comfortable always asking your husband to fill in for you, you can ask a friend or arrange with another mother to switch off taking care of each other's children. Always take advantage of sleep-overs and birthday parties. Don't always use this time to do dishes or wash floors. Relax, stay in your bathrobe after a bath, put an almond pack on your face, listen to some music, have some tea. Remember, too, that many places, such as health clubs, have inexpensive daycare services you can take advantage of.

Nothing has a stronger influence psychologically on their environment and especially on their children than the unlived life of the parent.

— Carl Jung

Another thing mothers can do to claim their own time, is to set firm bedtimes for their children. I know far too many mothers who, because they never established early bedtimes, never had time to read a book, listen to music, or talk to a friend or to their husbands in privacy, because the evening was spent taking care of children. As I mentioned in an earlier chapter, Peter and I tended to keep our girls up late because our travel schedules sometimes kept us away from them. But it is crucial that adult time be built into your day, and evening is one of your two best shots.

Doing Things with Grace

You know the feeling: Your children can't find their homework (even though it is right on their desks); your husband asks you where his glasses are; everyone acts as though they're helpless to do even the easiest things without your help. And this voice in your head says, *I must take care of this because I can, but why can't they just do it for themselves?* Before leaping to everyone's aid, check out your own needs. Try not to lose sight of yourself in all the demands of your children and your family. Do you have to do it all? What do you *need* to do? What do you *like* to do? Where do you draw the line and say, I cannot do this, I need time to myself?

You can become more mindful of your own needs by observing your moods as you do all the things you do for others. Women who become mothers are not expected to become martyrs, too. We shouldn't do anything for others that we can't do with grace.

Not long ago, I kissed Peter good-bye on his way out to a meeting. I noticed a loose button on the sleeve of his jacket. "Oops. You have a loose button." As irritating as it was that Peter's jacket had just arrived from the dry cleaner's in this condition, I popped out of my pretty, soothing bed, a pastel garden of pink, yellow, and blue-flowered sheets, padded down the hall to the linen closet, got out my sewing box, navigated some navy blue thread through a needle, sat down on the bed, and sewed the button tightly onto the jacket. Peter put it back on, kissed me a second time, and said, as he walked out the bedroom door, "I love you, darling. You're an angel. Thank you."

When you're able to take care of your own needs, when you can say *no* to others, you can do everything without feeling frustration, sensing that everyone is taking advantage of you.

> Treasure life in yourself and you give it to others; give it to others and it will come back to you. For life, like love, cannot thrive inside its own threshold but is renewed as it offers itself. Life grows as it is spent.
>
> — Ardis Whitman

You don't live in a world all alone.

— Dr. Albert Schweitzer

Sewing Peter's button took less than two minutes and was actually a pleasant interlude, even though it was an interruption. I had been reading, doing some research for a new book, and the break was refreshing. I appreciated the opportunity to do something small to show my love for Peter. We can find ways of being true to ourselves and nourish ourselves even when we're with our family.

A child is not a leech continuously sucking our identity from us. Children add meaning to everything we do in our lives; they should not be seen as taking anything away from us. But if we are feeling strung out, frantic, and pressured by others' demands, a loose button, or any other little household task, can be the last straw. It's when we do not tend to our own flowering that we feel drained by motherhood.

There is much strength in activating this nurturing, feminine side on our own behalf. As women, we have many ways to nourish our femininity that have nothing to do with attracting men or nurturing children. Our sensitivity, our ableness, our openness, and our pleasure in making life beautiful are traits that we love and are loved for. Men and women alike have a need both to nurture and to be taken care of. This is not a side of ourselves we should want to abandon, but rather should use in the service of everyone's needs, including our own.

Enriching Our Lives

I feel lucky to have discovered that some household tasks are therapeutic and satisfying outlets for creativity. I admit I love to iron — shirts, pillowcases, cloth napkins, tablecloths —

because to me, it's a very meditative and soothing activity. The rhythmic movement brings me solace.

I also enjoy painting things around the house because I love color. Recently, I looked at the bamboo design on the base of a tray table and decided the beige-brown color was dull. Painting it bright green picked up all the greens in the papier-mâché tray, making it look so much prettier.

There are endless ways to relax. Everyone is inspired by different things—you may not even be aware of all the things that move you. For example, you may find a renewed interest in plants and wildlife that you haven't felt since you visited the zoo as a child, and begin a hobby of bird watching or orchid growing. The wonderful fact is that you can always learn something new about yourself.

I met a woman recently who decided to take a mother-daughter painting class with her six-year-old. She found exhilaration working with red, yellow, and blue, and lots of white, mixing and experimenting, trying to avoid the pathetic mud color that occasionally resulted. A few weeks after starting the class, she told me that her daughter had caught her on the floor of the kitchen with a pair of large scissors in her hand and dozens of Matisse-like cutouts covering the floor—having the time of her life!

Charm is a glow within a woman that casts a most becoming light on others.

— John Mason Brown

There is no duty we so underrate as the duty of being happy.

— Robert Louis Stevenson

Broaden your interests If you haven't tried or simply haven't had the opportunity yet to broaden your life since becoming a mother, you may have to be clever in finding ways to keep your outside interests alive. One of the most gratifying things you can do is to educate yourself in something new. There's no reason to stop studying or learning just because you've finished school. Learning is a lifelong process. Sometimes we find we're open to understanding things we couldn't when we were younger. It's never too late to discover a new talent. I knew a woman who at the age of forty-three took her first drawing class and discovered that she was actually a fairly sophisticated artist. It has opened her life to new ways of expressing herself that she never even considered before.

No one ever gives us time. We never find time— we must seize time.

Seek out classes, lectures, poetry readings, and museum exhibitions. Go to jazz concerts, antique shops, art galleries, and botanical-garden shows. Try Chinese cooking lessons, a classic movie series, a beginning photography course. Visit an architecture library, go to the ballet—buy season tickets and then you *have* to go! Get in the habit of feeling comfortable doing things for yourself. If you spend all your time with family and close friends, you will inevitably deprive yourself of broadening and deepening your life. By regularly tending to your inner resources, your sense of self, you reach another level of awareness of the value of life, which helps you to set your priorities and discover what enlivens you.

Step out on your own If you are an extremely outgoing person, try to do at least two or three things a week by yourself. Even small "escapes" will allow you to gain enormous insights into your true self, insights that might otherwise be lost.

From time to time, I enjoy going to a nice restaurant alone.

What fun it can be to observe others, overhear bits of conversation, hear their laughter and soak up all the positive energy. There are times when I don't want to talk or be a good listener. When we're alone, we're free to muse, reflect, and center ourselves. Recently, I went alone to a favorite bistro on Madison Avenue for lunch. I dressed up, just for the pure pleasure of wearing something special. The French doors of the restaurant were thrown open so I sat in the sun and had a front-row seat for people-watching. As I looked at the parade of passersby, everyone seemed so spirited because of the sunshine. I emerged from my trance two hours later feeling massaged by angels.

Look for connections outside your role as mother The more interested you become in life, the more able you'll be to fill it with all manner of interesting people. You won't learn a whole lot sticking strictly to your own clan, your tight group of regular friends. They may be kindred souls, but remember, you have many different sides to your personality, and remaining close only to the people you know best doesn't allow you to be all you can be. Some of your friends may talk politics with great fluency but have little understanding of your love for historical novels and landscape painting. Other friends

Do you know what individuality is?... Consciousness of will. To be conscious that you have a will and can act.

– Katherine Mansfield

may love to share intimacies with you, but may not understand your pleasure in going to art lectures. You may feel frustrated at times when you are with old friends because certain aspects of your personality have no outlet when you are with them. Without realizing the cause, you may begin thinking that you simply no longer like your old friends, which probably isn't true. You just need to find some new ones.

> *The spirit within nourishes....*
>
> *— Virgil*

I had dinner recently with a woman in St. Louis who writes romantic novels. She wanted to make me one of the characters in her book. The only things we had in common were that we're women and we write. She wasn't interested in my family, but in me. I, in turn, added some color to her life. We had an amazingly good time together. She had assumed I would be a vision of bright lipstick, coiffed hair, and manicured nails and was refreshed to find me above all a down-to-earth mother who was serious about spirituality.

When you extend yourself to others and allow your energy to radiate freely, you enlarge your vision of yourself and the world. You learn how other people feel, what stirs their souls, what beliefs they hold, and how they live. Reaching out to others may just change your perception of your possibilities for yourself. I've met hundreds of fascinating people through my design work — both people in the trade and clients. My readers

> *The quality of learning...is within you, and it must come from the inside of your mind.*
>
> *— Lin Yutang*

are a great mix; some of them are particularly interesting because they are such free spirits. I have men and women friends who are actors, singers, artists, dancers, writers, sculptors, ministers, and teachers. I value having these friendships that are free from family connections. To them, I'm just Alexandra; not Peter's wife, not Alexandra and Brooke's mom. Seek and you shall find! These connections are out there waiting for you.

Read to commune with yourself and the world As mothers, we still need to grow spiritually, deepen emotionally, and find intellectual and creative outlets for our energies. Reading is one of my greatest pleasures. When we read good literature we are drawn into another world, often a higher, more resonant place. There we can experience life through another's consciousness. When we read we feel ourselves in the company of sages, soul mates even, and we feel we have entered into a timeless dialogue. Reading offers tremendous intimacy, a way to tap into things we feel but often find inexpressible. For these and so many other reasons, I feel that reading is as crucial to clearing my head as a good night's rest.

Cleaning your house while your kids are still growing/Is like shoveling the walk before it stops snowing.

— Phyllis Diller

I read with a ritualistic fervor. Every day, seven days a week, you can make a commitment to read a section of an inspiring book, an article, a sermon, or any other form of literature. Make the time. When you're raising kids, it often seems impossible to find this time but, trust me, it's there. I found it. You can wake up a little earlier than the rest of the family and sip a cup of coffee or tea and read. Or, you can retreat to bed at night a little earlier. Don't restrict your reading to flipping through the newspaper each morning at breakfast. Newspapers often bombard us relentlessly with bad or shocking news and don't provide us with much inspiration or reasons for joy. My daughter Brooke feels adamant about this. Recently, she grabbed *The New York Times,* looked at the pictures of dead bod-

Most things get better by themselves. Most things, in fact, are better by morning.

— Lewis Thomas

ies on the front page, and slapped it down on the kitchen table. "I'm not taking this paper to work. It's too depressing."

Always carry around something illuminating to read. There are usually moments, here and there, throughout the day—waiting in the dentist's office, in the car wash, or riding the bus—when you can read a bit. People often think I'm a student because I usually carry a tote bag filled with books and writing materials, which allows me to seize whatever spare time comes up. When I was an art student, I read Dostoyevsky on a crowded bus, standing up, holding a strap. If I had waited to read until I got a seat, I would have missed some great writing and some real opportunity for enlightenment.

As thy days, so shall thy strength be.

— Deuteronomy

Get your thoughts down on paper Many of us like to write, as well as to read. Some dream about writing a novel, memoir, or other nonfiction book. But too many of us put off writing until we "have the time." I assure you right now that there is never "enough time" to write. Fantasizing about escaping to an island to write your book or waiting until your family is all settled down will put very few words on paper. As with finding time to read, it's important to claim time every day, or at least regularly, to write.

In order to be in touch with someone else you must first be in touch with yourself.

— Michael J. Gelb

Before I wrote my first book, I made it a habit each day to sit in a chair, close my mouth and ears, and open my heart to write. I was frantic with raising two very active children—not an uncommon experience for most mothers—and found my writing time harder and harder to claim. I had to discipline myself to keep a daily journal. But once I set a regular pattern, I found that this addition to my schedule was actually a stress-reducer, rather than another burden. I was able to relax deeply in the moment, relieving the "anticipatory anxiety" about all the undone work in my life. Whether you keep a diary or write a few lines of poetry every day, try not to get into bed at night without writing. If you prefer to write a letter to a friend or a child who is away at college or camp, that's fine, just as long as you're putting thoughts down on paper. A writer friend had an English teacher at Barnard College in New York who told her students, "Write one page a day for three hundred and sixty-five days. At the end of the year, you'll have the equivalent of a book."

I believe that one has to have daily meditation. You must always dedicate half of the time to asking, and the other half to receiving the answer.

— Dr. Robert Wallis

Writing gives me the time to think about my life. I find that by pulling back in this way, I can see and embrace more. Writing gives me the chance to deepen my appreciation of my husband and children, my work, and my friends. Quiet time is not a luxury; it is as necessary to my life as food and sleep. Throughout my life I've found strength and inner peace from solitude. Writing is a very solitary act, but once you immerse yourself in it, an entire inner world is open to you.

Develop some measure of financial independence When I was a young mother, several women suggested that I quit my job so I could stay at home to raise my children. Some even asked, "Why can't you be happy being a wife and mother?" I

> *...the better you feel about yourself, the fewer limits you will place on your ability to love.*
>
> *— Judith Sills*

know this is a very delicate issue for many mothers. But how many people would ask a man, "Why can't you be happy being a husband and father?" without being laughed at or ignored. Now I realize that as women, we must each find our own truth, live it, breathe it, nourish it, and protect it, every day. My design work was a constant source of pleasure, satisfaction, and challenge. It stimulated me, fueled my passions, and gave me a greater appreciation about everything in my life.

But beyond my great fortune in having a career I loved, I learned one of the most useful lessons in life. In order to maintain the integrity of our independence and keep the flame of our own identity lit, it is helpful to have our own money. This is an observation that may make many at-home mothers uneasy. Although some mothers who do not work outside the home may have happily made the decision to stay home with their children, many probably still experience some anxiety about not having money that is entirely theirs to use at their own discretion. Many women have told me that although they have never regretted their choice not to work outside the home, it is very difficult not having their own money. What's the remedy for this very prevalent situation?

The most obvious answer is to earn your own money. This may be "easier said than done," but today there are more options for earning money by working at home. A mother can be a freelance writer, for example. She could also make ceramics or paint watercolors and sell them to local stores or studios, many of which will display and sell new art. But you don't need to be a talented writer or artist to earn money.

Outside the home, you could work in a local bookstore, where you'll be surrounded by great books, or in a clothing store. Look through the job listings in your local paper. The jobs, many of which involve sales, may not be glamorous, but are rewarding nonetheless. The goal isn't to find your life's calling in a job, but to give you a greater sense of freedom by making your own money.

Earning your own money can be extremely restorative, even if it is only a small amount each week. In my early career, I eventually made the transition from earning enough money to support my two daughters to being able to make enough money to take them on trips. In both scenarios, earning my own money added to my contentment. Even if you choose to do a lot of volunteer work, you can establish a balance between working for a charity and working for money part-time. Not only will this extra money come in handy in meeting household expenses, but you can use it for your own personal wants, without having to justify your spending to anybody. Though there is nothing wrong with putting aside a percentage of the household budget for your own discretionary use, many mothers are uncomfortable with this practice. If this is the case with you, make an effort to earn money. You may find that the time adjustments you have to make are minor compared to the rewards. In a culture that runs on money, money gives us more of the freedoms that we are entitled to.

Actions, thoughts, and feelings which are conducive to the proper functioning and unfolding of our total personality produce a feeling of inner approval, of "rightness" characteristic of the humanistic "good conscience."

— Erich Fromm

Keeping Your Inner Garden Colorful

In his book *Hua Hu Chung,* the ancient Eastern philosopher Lao-tzu wrote about attaining enlightenment and mastery: "Those who want to know the truth of the universe should practice the four cardinal virtues: The first is reverence for all life; this manifests as unconditional love and respect for oneself and all other beings."

The spirit of truth and the spirit of freedom...

— Henrik Ibsen

Indeed, without unconditional love and respect for ourselves we will not have those same gifts to offer to our children. There must be time for breaks from the unavoidable stress and tedium of raising a family. Some mothers are so stressed out and overextended they even fear taking any time at all for themselves. Have they given away more than they have? Are they afraid to be alone long enough to face their inner selves? When we shed all the excuses we make for not having time for ourselves, when we shed all the "shoulds" and "musts" of mothering, we can sit down, have a cup of tea, and take a moment to come to ourselves. Like the rainbow after a rainstorm, when you take this time for yourself your anxiety begins to subside and something beautiful rises up: yourself.

Your own gift can present every moment with the cumulative force of a whole life's cultivation....

— Emerson

To the illuminated, *now* feels so delicious. When we place value on our individuality and on our inner growth and learn to recognize our own emotional needs, we can nourish and serve our separate souls with time and tranquility, spiritual teachings, meditation, solitude, stillness, and a rich variety of involvements. Doing so helps us to remain strong inside and out. I can stretch my arms out wide, embrace this space, and fill it with meaning. When we open ourselves to ourselves, we remain juicy and our inner garden stays colorful, generous, and loving. What better gift can we give our children than ourselves in all our glory?

Chapter 5

Enjoying Time with Each Other

*Mother...you must never go
down to the end of the town
if you don't go down with me.*

—A. A. Milne

From the very first time your newborn child lights up to a brightly colored toy or fixes her gaze on the smiling faces around her, she's expressing that wonderful human urge to play. Waving a rattle in her face or speaking to her in high-pitched tones will elicit coos and laughter. These heavenly sounds are perhaps the clearest expression of the pure delight and pleasure we can have in the world. As young as she is, your child has already begun to learn about some of the playfulness that is in store for her in the future.

Your child's natural instinct is to have fun, to explore, to make believe, and to be industrious in that play. Whether she is on the kitchen floor playing jacks, making a dollhouse out of a cardboard box, or playing basketball, through the wonder and delight of this play your child learns about the world and how to navigate her way through it.

While we, on the other hand, might be bogged down by bills

> Between the dark and the daylight,/ When the night is beginning to lower,/ Comes a pause in the day's occupations/ That is known as the Children's Hour.
>
> — Henry Wadsworth Longfellow

to pay or dinners to cook, our children's spontaneity and greed for pleasure remind us of what it is like to live in the moment. In joining them, we learn that we, too, can still be spontaneous.

I've always had lots of fun with children. Regardless of age or personality, whether they're shy or spirited, I love to enter their imaginary worlds and teach them something about mine, too. Whether I'm with a newborn baby who smiles brilliantly back at me or with a four-year-old who allows me to change her doll's diapers, I'm glad to be with this little dreamer. Children vibrate with imagination and their play is vivid and authentic. When I'm with children, I'm uninhibited, playful, and simply glad to be in their company. Who wouldn't be?

When our children invite us to play, it doesn't matter what we're doing, we should drop it. Chances are that the time you spend together will be memorable. Our ability to drop everything and play fills our children with love and happiness. What can open our children's hearts wider than adults who respond to their call to play at any given moment? I feel like a child whenever, in a spontaneous fit of passion, I ask Peter to dance with me. Sometimes, surprised by the suddenness of the invitation, he hesitates and begins to say, "Later, not now." But once it becomes clear to him that this is a special moment that cannot be retrieved once lost, he gladly, even eagerly, joins in. This is what children ask of us, and when we give it to them, we get a lot more back for ourselves. Children are constant reminders of how good life can be. They love the plain and simple. An ice cream cone will do just fine as the topping to a great day in the playground.

We may be so wrapped up in planning our

Childhood is a blissful time of play and fantasizing, of uninhibited sensual delight.

— Clare Boothe Luce

lives that we miss these opportunities for living. But the honey, the real-life treats, can be found largely in these detours off our straight-and-narrow path. These are the times when the unexpected can happen. Some of the most memorable times Peter and I shared with Alexandra and Brooke were the result of their ideas. They instinctively knew how to make the most of a moment. They always seemed to know what to do next. "Let's all go to Baskin Robbins and get bubble gum ice cream cones." "Let's go for a bike ride on a bicycle-built-for-two." "Let's pack a picnic so after the zoo we can have dinner in the park." "Let's sunbathe by the fountain at the Seagram Building." "Let's go ice skating."

So many worlds, so much to do, so little done, such things to be.

— Alfred, Lord Tennyson

The simplest things can become a delicious adventure with our children. I remember what a joy it was to take Alexandra and Brooke to school. After dropping them off, I would run to my job as a decorator. These moments we would spend together before the girls joined their friends at school were times when we were free to be. Each of us appreciated the interlude. For several years, we lived twenty blocks from school and we always had to decide whether to walk or take the bus. If we walked we were usually tempted to stop at Jimmy's on Madison Avenue and Eighty-third

My mother had a great deal of trouble with me, but I think she enjoyed it.

— Mark Twain

Street to get a glass of fresh orange juice or cup of hot chocolate. I was always game for a cup of tea or coffee, sharing a corn muffin, and kissing the sweet marmalade off my child's lips. Only a mother can lick the chocolate off her child's face when she doesn't have a handkerchief.

There is so much to enjoy about raising our children. I miss the red galoshes and the shiny quilted blue snowsuits marching along in a happy cadence; the yellow pajamas with the feet on them that snap up the front and were the costume after the bath. I miss the colorful illustrated notes my girls pinned on their bedroom doors with messages of love and lots of XOXOXOs. I miss our painting sessions, when we'd sit at the kitchen table with our huge pads of white paper and share a pot of Magic Markers and colored pencils. We'd make several paintings in one sitting, playing with color and form. Often we'd do watercolors, using simple, inexpensive paint boxes containing bright primary colors. Brooke enjoyed acrylics. When she was seven years old, she sold her first painting for twenty dollars to a client of mine in Tennessee whose house I was decorating. Shelly displayed Brooke's small lily-of-the-valley canvas in the living room on an easel alongside the work of artists who were more established, but who I'm not certain were any more artistic.

Wonder implies the desire to learn; the wonderful is therefore the desirable.

— Aristotle

Where does our creativity begin? I remember doing watercolors on an easel in our sunroom in Westport, Connecticut, with my mother as she worked on sculpting a bust in clay. These daily art sessions led to a passionate interest in color, form, composition, and design. When Brooke needed a painting to go on a large wall opposite her antique campaign bed, she bought a large canvas and painted a scene of Provence. It seemed the natural thing for her to do. Ever since she was seven and used her twenty dollars to buy more canvases, she has delighted in painting with acrylics and oils. We used to tease her when she'd come back from church on Sunday and want to paint in her best dress, too eager to change clothes. Often she goes in her bedroom in Stonington, shuts the two doors, and, in her own world, works on several canvases at once. Over the years, the paint palette has become more elaborate, but her artistic vision remains pure. She loves to express light and vibrancy in clear, pure colors. It all began with our kitchen-table paintfests.

I miss holding my little ones in my lap by the warm glow of a crackling fire reading all my favorite childhood books which they also cherished. I miss hunting for mica in the sand at the playground, doing somersaults on the lawn, decorating their rooms with them, helping them grow plants in their indoor window boxes, and helping each of them to create a secret place to go be alone.

I miss my girls taking turns over who would sit next to me at breakfast, lunch, and dinner. I miss our nature walks in the early spring, discovering the first forsythia and a host of daffodils smiling brightly in the warm, fragrant spring air. I miss the trips to the flower shop, the ice cream store, and the bakery. I miss hanging out in the library at the children's tables, sitting on brightly painted little chairs. I miss the beach days, the swim meets, the ribbons. I miss the train trips, the car rides, the buses, and the airplanes. I miss raking leaves and climbing the hill to the apple orchard to pick apples in October for making applesauce and pies together. I miss having the girls decorate the cheese platter when friends came over,

When a child plays, he is the manipulator; he makes do with whatever is at hand. His imagination transforms the commonplace into the priceless. A wooden clothespin, rescued from under the kitchen table and wrapped in a dishcloth, becomes a baby; a penny thrust under a cushion becomes a buried treasure.

— Eda LeShan

and then serve the hors d'oeuvres to our guests. In their long, Laura Ashley flowered dresses and with shining clean hair, they glowed with pride in their family.

Small opportunities are often the beginning of great enterprises.

— Demosthenes

These princesses who dressed up in my clothes and put on my shoes when they were little, gradually grew into them. The spun-silk hair that I loved braiding and tying with pastel plaid ribbons now cascades over their shoulders. My babies are now young ladies. I thank my lucky stars that I could participate with them in their childhood adventures. I'm grateful we made every moment count when we were together.

When we're confident with each other — child to mother and vice versa, as well as in all relationships — we soften. When we open up our hearts to our children, like a dancer, we bend to their rhythms with greater ease and less effort. Whenever I was with the girls I felt I was a more highly evolved person. Loving them and being such a central part of their world expanded and clarified my own life. I was continuously renewed. My attention was undivided and my belief in them unshakable. They taught me that though the mind acquires knowledge, the heart balances it with understanding. During those private times, because no one disturbed our peace, nothing seemed to agitate us. We didn't struggle; we held hands tightly in a gesture of intense love.

Mothers at Work

Whether you are a mother working at home keeping your house in order or if you also have a job or career, taking the time to play and enjoy your children can be a tricky balancing act. In *Living Beautifully Together,* I suggested we time-tithe, spending 90 percent of our waking time helping others, giving of ourselves in some capacity, and 10 percent of our time in self-renewal, resurrection, regeneration, and nourishment to the soul. As mothers, such a large portion of our time is spent in support of our children. Is it possible that we can benefit from some time-tithing here, too? Can we not allocate 10 percent of our caring and nurturing time for our children solely to have fun and play? Absolutely!

During the two years I spent as a single, working, divorced mother I always had to choose my priorities and make sure I planned ahead, if I wanted to do what I needed to do and have fun, too. We all do, otherwise chaos would overcome us. As we make up our schedules to fit in everything, we have to keep in mind that what's important in the long run is not keeping up with the endless chores, but those carefree moments when we drop whatever we're doing and connect with our child. Of course we must deal with the everyday necessities of running a home; it's a boring nuisance to run out of dishwashing liquid or toilet paper, orange juice or coffee, and have to make a special trip to the market. But, on the other hand, if we are too organized, too programmed to the point where we allow no room for occasional diversions, we risk tuning out a great deal of the beautiful music we can share with our children.

It is extremely important for mothers who work to make sure that their time with their children is focused on their

> *No child should grow up unaware of the dawn chorus of the birds in spring.*
>
> — Rachel Carson

> *Youth had been a habit of hers for so long, that she could not part with it.*
>
> — Rudyard Kipling

togetherness, not on their next appointment. I often had to be careful not to get involved in unnecessary social entanglements that would complicate my life. I worked extremely hard at my job and when I was free to be with my children, I tried to have as few distractions as possible.

When I bring you colored toys, my child, I understand why there is such a play of colors in clouds, on water, and why flowers are painted in tints.

— Rabindranath Tagore

In the space I made for them I found a wonderful openness and directness in our relationship. While they enjoyed their play dates with friends, those private, shared times with me were essential for their self-confidence. Our growing respect and love for one another made us even more certain that the time we had set aside for enjoyment was well worth it. I poured myself into being with them. How did I know what to do? I just took my cues from Alexandra and Brooke. We followed each other to a wonderful place.

When I was working and raising the girls I often found that each of my dual roles taught me about the other. Comparing them also offered an interesting study in opposites. Here I was, decorator extraordinaire, all dressed up in a silk dress and blazer, a silk snood to top it off, and a pair of white kid gloves in my hand. I'd take the girls to school in my smashing work costume, kiss them good-bye, and off I'd go to work, several blocks down the street. At midday, I'd escape work and pick them up at school. Together we'd skip home, where I would shed my formality, put on a T-shirt and white shorts, and run up to our roof to play. I'd painted everything white and put down green astro turf. We'd grill hamburgers for lunch, sunbathe, play, and simply be together. This was our secret place where I was queen and the girls were princesses. There was no telephone, so I could not be reached (unlike today, when you can be reached in the middle of the Atlantic Ocean!). I refused to tell anyone about this special time; it was our secret.

The opportunity for doing mischief is found a hundred times a day....

— Voltaire

After this dreamy time I'd bathe, slip back into my formal clothes, kiss the girls good-bye as they headed off for their afternoon naps. Their "work" day was over at 12:30. The mother's helper I had stayed with them when I went back to work and they napped. Back at work, my eyes twinkled with my concealed delights. I was operating covertly as the only decorator at the firm who was also raising small children. I kept this quiet for fear of jeopardizing my position there. Those were the days when women who worked were put on what was called the "mommy track," which means a path going nowhere. Are we still in the same place? Thank God, some changes have been made in that perception. Back then, I was all business, getting my job done as fast as possible so I could be with the girls again.

I wasn't always so clear on how to set my priorities. I remember when I started my own firm I would pay a baby-sitter to take them to do fun things outside the apartment, things I wanted to be doing with them myself. I got smart one day and realized that instead of paying someone to stay with the girls while I prepared dinner and straightened the house, I could pay someone else to peel potatoes, do the wash, iron, make beds, and clean the house so I could have adventures with the girls.

No matter how busy a mother you are, you've got to find that 10 percent of time to have fun. A friend who has a five-year-old asked me once, "How do you find time to have all these good times with your girls?" I looked Brenda in the eye and answered, "You don't find the time, you seize the moment. You *take* the time."

Finding Zen Time

Taking time to enjoy our children requires that we change our perception of time and what is supposed to take place within it. When we can stop seeing time as being only a space in which to get things done, we can also give up the illusion that once things are done we have arrived at completion. When we give that up, we realize that nothing will ever be perfect and therefore we can use time in which to experience our lives rather than to make our lives chug along. Redefining time connects us to experiences that will make our time richer.

> *Let early education be a sort of amusement; you will then be better able to find out the natural bent.*
>
> — *Plato*

In his book *The Spirit of Zen,* Alan W. Watts, a longtime student and teacher of Zen Buddhism, teaches us a lot about how time is perceived from a Zen perspective. He helps us to "flow by the stream of events, for it goes forward with the stream and becomes one with it...there is nothing at all which one can hold on to and say, 'This is it; I have got it.'"

Watts teaches us that Zen is founded on an "intimate, personal experience" and assures us that "it will be a joy inexpressible." Rather than being overly concerned about the passage of time, we need to focus on what's happening moment by moment. There is no exact time when we suddenly become enlightened. Being alive to the moment is key to Zen and to being a mother. There's no such thing as enjoying time with each other in haste.

Raising my children gave me direct contact with the truth of Zen. There was wisdom in the paths we took together, my girls and I. They were the leaders. Like the Zen masters, my girls "can never explain," they "can only indicate." All children can be Zen masters, because they know so well how to live fully in the moment. The Zen master would have his student look at the cherry blossom. Alexandra and Brooke would take me to the cherry tree, sit me down beneath it, and settle in my lap. I'd lean my head against the tree. Experiencing this was Zen Nirvana.

My lifelong friend Wendy sent me a letter of sympathy after my older brother Powell's death. She spoke of our memories of the past: "For the most part our families provided us with a golden childhood. It was later, out in the real world, that we started to get pushed around—often from pillar to post. I've often thought it would be fun to escape to that moment or two in time when we felt safe, if only to rest awhile."

Resting in our place is what Zen teaches us. But so much in our life takes us away from the place of calm. When I was raising my daughters, I was constantly battling against my outside duties. Alexandra and Brooke drew me out of my world of schedules and preoccupations and brought me into their world, where I lost all sense of chronological time. It was there that I could shed my adult burdens for a while and enter into a realm of pure experience. I was intoxicated with

There is no problem in the world that cannot be solved with a story.

— Witch doctor of the Xhosa tribe, South Africa

The walks and talks we have with our two-year-olds in red boots have a great deal to do with the values they will cherish as adults.

— Edith F. Hunter

But Mr. Jeremy liked getting his feet wet; nobody ever scolded him, and he never caught a cold.

— Beatrix
Potter

pure bliss. This was a second childhood for me because I was truly connected with my daughters on their level.

I played *their* games. They were in charge. The girls taught me their rules, which gave me insight into their vast imaginations. Like Alice in Wonderland, I became absorbed in their reality, swept up in the thrill of going down a slide, not once, not twice, but maybe twenty times, falling into sand, giggling, making sand castles, playing tag, hide-and-seek, dressing up in costumes, pretending we owned a grocery store or dress shop. We played house, we baked, we decorated gingerbread houses, we turned cardboard boxes into fantasy houses. They carefully planned what they wanted to engage me in next and there was never a dull moment. While I was at work, they'd plot the path for highly charged fun time together.

Whether we put a puzzle together, played cards, strung beads, played checkers, or made collages, we were industrious, active, and happy.

Seizing the Moment

There were days when I felt the household had too strong a grasp on me and I didn't know how to take pleasure with the girls. Is this only a female condition? Most of us want our homes to run well, to be beautiful, comfortable, and well ordered. But when I felt this urge was becoming a compulsion that trapped me, I would take off my apron and other strings, and escape the apartment with Alexandra and Brooke in tow. We need to seize the moment or we will be seized by it. When

I physically left the apartment I felt free: no phone interruptions, no household chores waiting for me to do.

What a blessing to experience these exhilarating moments of play with our children! Whenever I entered the girls' world, everything seemed so effortless. No one bossed us around. No one even knew where we were. Sometimes we weren't sure ourselves where we were or where we were going. We were open to whatever seemed interesting at the time. If we weren't in the mood for dinner at home, we'd follow our cravings to Kentucky Fried Chicken or a pizza joint. The harried feelings I had felt earlier in the day lifted, and I wanted to be no place other than where we were.

You probably have experienced this sense of putting your "to-do" lists aside and going with the flow. These feel like peak experiences; the sensation that you have arrived at some simple, yet perfect, moment. Even if you're taking your 3,650th trip to the playground, there can be freshness each time, if you are open to it. You can go to the children's zoo, where you and your children can delight in learning every animal by name.

> *Even when freshly washed and relieved of all obvious confections, children tend to be sticky.*
>
> *— Fran Lebowitz*

> *Ah, what is more blessed than to put cares away!*
>
> *— Gaius Valerius Catullus*

The Magic of Unstructured Play

Many mothers, including myself, raise their children unlike how their parents raised them, including how they play. When

I was growing up, I basically did what I was told to do. Mother would announce we were off to Weston to visit our young cousins, and all four children would jump in the car—even though we'd rather be doing something else. When I had Alexandra and Brooke, I decided to have a good time a different way—their way. I did what they wanted to do. Time and time again, we'd end up laughing hysterically over some inside joke, some shared experience. These are some of my favorite memories. I think the key to this magic connection was that our time together was unstructured. We could leave the apartment to go on some spontaneous adventure in the park or we could play indoors and do a project together. If they were in the mood to bake cupcakes and decorate them, that's what we did. Or we'd dye Easter eggs, make Christmas ornaments, or decorate boxes, redecorate their room, or rearrange their books in the library. There was never any stridency or emphasis on efficiency or accomplishments; rather, there was a sense of adventure, ideally timed to suit their moods. Once I was 100 percent available for them, I loved the surprises and serendipity of going along with their energetic proposals, an undertaking usually requiring a concerted effort. They never had little schemes in mind, and their excitement was always infectious.

You must wake and call me early, call me early, mother dear; Tomorrow'll be the happiest time of all the glad New Year—

— Alfred, Lord Tennyson

We took walks around Central Park to see the burst of spring in the flowering apple blossoms. We had June picnics and bike rides. We sipped Shirley Temples at hotel restaurants and tea at the Plaza Palm Court. We'd go to Chock full o'Nuts for powdered doughnuts, and ride the carousel in Central Park to catch the golden ring. Rain or shine, we'd be out and about. We took art classes and went to museum exhibitions. At the Met, we'd toss coins in the fountain and make huge wishes. Even buying shoes was, and still is, a treat. We went to the movies and to plays. At Christmastime, we went to see the lighting of the tree at Rockefeller Center. We went to see Tchaikovsky's remarkable *Nutcracker* ballet. All three of us enjoyed ourselves so much during these "pure play" times; they were tremendous fun, but also made us feel all warm and cozy inside.

> *He was such an inoffensive little boy, she could find no fault with him, except his tendency to disappear.*
>
> — *Colette*

Many parents flee the city in favor of raising their children in a safer, less stressful environment. I'm grateful that our daughters grew up in New York City. I don't think they'd have traded this experience for the world. They attended an excellent school and made friends with a diverse group of people. We enjoyed all the benefits a vital city has to offer, including a beautiful park, a wonderful children's zoo—half a block from our apartment—the American Museum of Natural History, and a huge array of creative opportunities.

> *The essence of pleasure is spontaneity.*
>
> — *Germaine Greer*

When we left the city for vacations, we'd have a great time, too. I fully participated in every game, each activity. Merely watching would be to miss out. We'd play croquet, tether ball, and basketball. We'd race each other, fly kites, collect seashells, climb trees, and go on scavenger hunts. We did somersaults and tumbled together down grassy hills.

The girls taught me to be awake and alert, to listen and stay open. When they were teenagers, we'd often end up poking around in thrift shops in Greenwich Village. We always explored the fun antique shops everywhere. We especially liked going to Pierre Deux on Bleecker Street. The girls were constantly exposed to a variety of fascinating things and interesting people. These grooves were forays into new exciting terrain.

> *...consent to feel like a child & attain to seeing like a seer....*
>
> *— Elizabeth Barrett Browning*

When I was young, I had an art teacher who would take us on outings and had to remind us to look up at the buildings, sculptures, trees, and sky. My girls naturally looked in all directions, flexible and curious about everything. One December Saturday, we found ourselves at Saks Fifth Avenue. As soon as we got through the revolving door, Brooke announced that she was hungry. She wanted a cheeseburger. Alexandra and I laughed, and the three of us revolved ourselves right out of there. We made it to Hamburger Heaven well before the noon crowd and had a fun early lunch party. Wherever our journey took us, we always anticipated a good experience.

> *Some of my best friends are children. In fact, all of my best friends are children.*
>
> *— J. D. Salinger*

Years ago, I had an exercise teacher who was a dancer and choreographer. One day Liz told me that the difference between herself and "most people our age, Alexandra, is that I kept dancing through life and most adults forget how to move their bodies." Along with Liz, the girls helped me remember to dance. Liz was grace itself. She'd sing out, skip, and chant, *cha, cha, cha*. She seemed to me a woman half her age. Between Liz and the girls, my body stayed fit and flexible.

I loved the city as the setting for my children's childhood. Even though the view from their bedroom window wasn't of gardens and trees, they were exposed to a wealth of experiences that they now treasure. The city played an important role in my girls' development and values.

Being a working mother also presented opportunities for activities I might enjoy with my children—some of them very unconventional. For example, I often took my children with me to see clients. This way I could be near them while they played with clients' children or

Children's playings are not sports and should be deemed as their most serious actions.

— Michel de Montaigne

were treated to the cookie jar and ice cream. I always took them shopping with me, whether I was buying clothes for them or for myself, or decorations and supplies for the apartment. Even today, we adore going shopping together. We never hurry. One of these special, spur-of-the-moment excursions can last an hour or three. They continue to fill me with happiness.

Enjoying Time with Adult Children

"Hey, Mom, let's go for a walk." When I hear this, my apron is off and I'm running to ring the elevator in our apartment building or jump down the steps of our cottage. Whenever we are invited to join our grown-up child in an activity, it's bound to be a heartfelt experience. Many of my happiest, most treasured moments with Alexandra and Brooke have been these surprise occasions when I'm invited to participate with them in some activity. I'm there without a second thought, because whatever we do together is memorable.

*A child's world
is fresh and new
and beautiful, full
of wonder and
excitement.*

— Rachel Carson

Last year, Brooke invited me to take a ceramics class with her. We made dessert and dinner plates for a mutual friend who was getting married. After several hours working on a project together, I felt we had experienced an evening that linked so many earlier ones, filling me with nostalgia. When we joined Peter for a late supper, we were all bubbling over. He loved seeing us so animated and said, "Next time you go, may I join you? You sound as though you had such a good time."

We still make play dates to go to the park, sit at the boathouse, and have a cool drink. We make lunch dates at a favorite restaurant, go for a walk on a beach, get massages at Stressless Steps, take pictures of one another, go to a museum exhibition, meet after work for a drink or dinner. Or we'll do a painting project or go to a lecture or movie.

That tender, happy trip to Paris we all took after my brother Powell died ended up being a healing experience for all of us. Whenever we, as a family, are far away from our jobs and friends, we're isolated in time and space, thrown back into the wonderful days when the girls were growing up. In those days we had regular times together that were sacrosanct and inviolable.

Today, Peter loves it whenever the three Stoddard women ditch him in order to continue our traditional rituals. I find that shopping without the girls is perfunctory and lacks spark. On one of our afternoon jaunts in Paris, Alexandra and Brooke invited me to a wonderful French department store to look at shoes, hats, scarves, and dresses. Before I knew what was happening, they were finding things for me—a delphinium-blue wool shawl to wrap over a coat or suit, velvet at-home slippers, fuchsia rubbers for gardening—and, when we landed on the floor that sold women's suits, the big idea came to me. This was the moment to seize: *Carpe momentum!* We would each select a new spring suit. The fun we each had trying on suits, bringing one another different cuts and colors into the dressing room, was boundless. After several happy hours in the department store, we flaunted our shopping bags to Peter when we met him for an espresso at a café. He suggested we wear our new costumes to dinner, which we did with great delight, primping longer than usual beforehand. We were thrilled to have rekindled the memories of the shopping sprees we'd had when the girls were younger. We are friends. We have loads of fun together, and our grooves continue to sew the years into a beautiful tapestry.

> *Make-believe colors the past with innocent distortion, and it swirls ahead of us in a thousand ways—It is part of our collective lives, entwining our past and our future…*
> *a particularly rewarding aspect of life itself.*
> — Shirley Temple Black

We also still have wonderful family parties. Recently, Alexandra hosted a celebration with seven of her best friends. She invited Peter and me to join them for drinks before they went out to dinner. What is the secret that allows some families to nurture one another and maintain genuine rapport? We find we still enjoy being together as a family. It would break my heart if Alexandra and Brooke spent time with us out of obligation. I believe in the sanctity, the holiness of family life. When there is this genuine caring and love, the mutual support is truly uplifting. I know many families who insist on regular command performances, specific times when everyone is expected to appear, regardless of personal or extenuating circumstances. When parents make a child feel indebted to them out of sense of duty, the magical connection disappears. Children can and often do go through the motions of caring, using manners to mask their feelings, often afraid not to show up for these prescribed family reunions. In all the years Peter and I have been married, I only remember him once asking his grown daughters, Andrée and Blair, to come to an event with a "Please, do it—for me" added to the invitation. Because he normally never says this, his daughters took it very seriously and we were all together for an especially important family conclave. When our children are invited to join us at a celebration, we extend a genuine invitation. If the timing isn't right or if for any other reason a child chooses not to come, we must respect that. Why ruin a good thing? Adult children have more burdens on their time than we do. They work extremely hard, long hours, and often don't have a great deal of flexibility at their jobs. Rather than planning special occasions that are locked into specific dates, perhaps it would be best to check with your child beforehand.

Now that Alexandra lives in Washington, she can't make it to many of our New York celebrations. She often works until ten o'clock and comes home exhausted and goes straight to bed. Coming to New York during the week is too tiring. Rather than being disappointed, we make other plans. She loves it when we

...you can enjoy these riches every day of your life.

— Walt Disney

Once upon a time there were four little Rabbits, and their names were—Flopsy, Mopsy, Cottontail, and Peter

— Beatrix Potter

go to see her in Washington. When love is shared, there's always a way to find a place and a convenient time to be together. When our children are ready, we're there. Alexandra and Brooke know that, which thrills me.

Age has nothing to do with this relationship. I know a ten-year-old daughter who is simpatico with her mother, and I feel certain they will continue to be close all their lives. When there is a sense of interactiveness, when you maintain and nurture a sincere, dynamic, continuously vital, vigorous, active interest in what each of you is doing, you sympathize with each other, sharing and understanding feelings and ideas. You're favorably inclined, you feel and express compassion, and are in harmonious accord. We continue to keep up this rapture, this pleasure with our children because the relationship is based on a combination of sincere and active interest in one another. Alexandra, Brooke, and I constantly check in with each other: "What's going on?" "How's Peter?" "What's new?" We care about what each of us is doing, thinking, and feeling, in the context of our separate lives.

In the novel *Light* by Eva Figes, when painter Claude Monet's step-granddaughter Lily let her brother Jimmy play, in the garden at Giverny after lunch, with her red balloon purchased by an aunt from a vagabond, Jimmy let go of the string at the kitchen door. When Lily complained, crying out, "I've lost my balloon!" a friend of hers said confidentially, "That's the only way to keep a balloon—by letting it go. Didn't you know that?"

> *Children themselves do not sentimentalize childhood, and they see nothing uncanny in it.*
>
> — Walter Kendrick

> *Pooh hasn't much brain, but, he does silly things and they turn out right.*
>
> — A. A. Milne

Monet added, "He's right, you know?" Then Lily heard him say quietly, "You wait and see." We can't win people's attention and affection any more than we can cling tightly to a balloon. We need to let our loved ones fly away from us, so the world will benefit from their wonderful selves. As Claude Monet assured Lily about her balloon, "It might drift, in which case lots of people will see it, all over the country."

> *Inspiration comes to those who inspire.*
>
> *– Peter Megargee Brown*

What is the secret of continuing family connection and joy? When we keep the door open (in both directions), children will gladly want to visit. When our home is a place where our children feel at one with themselves, with the spirit and power of place, and where they feel a deep sense of belonging, we will always be together. When returning home makes us feel better for the visit, we are blessed. Being together willingly, with a sense of appreciation and gladness, enjoying each other's company, is the best life has to offer. We make these special dates to celebrate each other. I admit I'm sappy about this continuity, but how can I help it when I feel such rich rewards from our mutual love and respect?

Practical Playtime

When children are young, you are generally very busy. Not only was I a working mother, but after more than a decade together, my first husband and I divorced, which meant the girls spent lots of time away from me with their dad on vacations in California or on ski holidays. These periods of separation only made me more aware of the preciousness of our time

We also loved to create Chinese banquets in our wok. We'd peel and chop carrots, onions, and snow peas, and put them all in individual clear glass bowls before mixing them together in the wok with a touch of oil, soy sauce, and lemon juice. We'd add a few cherry tomatoes and parsley as a final touch and serve these vegetables with a rosemary chicken I had already roasted. The smells were juicy and sweet and filled the whole kitchen with their rich aromas. I'd have sliced lemons, limes, and oranges at the table to bite into between conversation and swallows.

The child amidst his baubles, is learning the action of light, motion, gravity, muscular force; and in the game of human life, love, fear, justice, appetite, man, and God, interact.

— Emerson

On some Chinese nights we'd cheat. No one cooked, but we'd set up exotic table decorations, using black lacquer bowls and the red chopsticks I brought back from my trip around the world. We were lucky because some of the best take-out Chinese food outside of China is within delivery distance from our New York apartment. One of my editors for whom I was writing freelance articles at *Reader's Digest*, Eleanor Prouty, thought the girls and I always cooked our Chinese food for our Wednesday night feasts. What a laugh we had when I told her it arrived 100 percent prepared at our kitchen door—everything from the wonton soup to the fortune cookies. So even when we didn't cook with the wok or prepare food together, mealtime was always an exciting adventure.

In preparing the table, we'd jointly choose the colors, the candles, flowers, and decor. Every meal in our family, including breakfast, was attractively served. We did these things to uplift *us*, to bring light and color and joy to our daily lives together.

together. I wanted to make every second count. The groov
where we left the apartment to explore the world became eve
more sacrosanct. At home, where there are always practica
chores, the girls participated naturally in the gentle rhythms ol
domestic life. I found hundreds of ways to involve them with
what I was doing.

There is something absolutely delicious about creating
meaningful rituals around our domestic chores with our children, particularly cooking. Cooking was something we did
together as a family. In the kitchen we could all be together,
preparing a banquet each of us would especially enjoy. I
learned to ask the girls what they felt like cooking and eating,
so that everyone really felt like an integral part of the process.
When we cooked together I realized how rea-
sonable their tastes were. There was always an
emphasis on wholesome, nutritious food. I
allowed the girls to acquire taste for food gradually, never forcing either of them to eat a bite
they didn't want.

*How many young
geniuses we have
known.*

— Emerson

We cherished every aspect of cooking and
eating together. We loved to boil artichokes in
our huge white pot. There is something won-
derfully liberating about *having* to use your hands when you eat
artichokes. We'd put out little dishes of garnishes and sauces —
lemon wedges, chopped parsley, rock salt, cracked ground
pepper, Dijon mayonnaise, vinaigrette, and soy sauce into
which we'd dip each leaf. The plates we selected for the artichokes and accompaniments were equal in importance to the
food. Years later, Alexandra and Brooke still get a kick out of
remembering these decorative, vivid dishes we used for our
mealtime ceremonies.

When it came time to do the dishes, Alexandra loved the "water play." After these cozy, enjoyable family dinners she found pleasure in putting the kitchen back into shipshape order. Water running, talking on the phone with a friend, she'd wash, scrub, polish, and put away the dishes.

Children display tremendous vitality and rush at every day with open arms.

— Dr. Deepak Chopra

Aside from cooking and cleaning up after meals, we had fun doing a host of household tasks. When I ironed, the girls would prepare the clean linens and clothing by first sorting them into categories—shirts, pillowcases, napkins—and then hand them to me one by one for the spray starch and the ironing. Often while I was ironing, they would sit with me and paint and draw at the kitchen table. I'd stack the starched, neatly folded napkins in piles and the girls would select colorful, festive ribbons to tie the bundles together.

When it came time to polish the furniture, brass, copper, and silver, the whole family would gleefully pitch in. Alexandra and Brooke, like their mother, loved the challenge of making things shine! The hours they spent in antique stores with me inspired them to polish everything in sight. When we had finished our spree, we'd see our home in a "new light."

Ta-ra-ra-boom-de-ay!

— Henry J. Sayers

Young children, too, enjoy participating in domestic chores. Sometimes the most fun a kid can have is washing the floors with you. Don't overlook any opportunity for play; it can be found everywhere.

Building Your Child's Confidence Through Play

Children love to make decisions and to be taken seriously. When a mother asks her child, "What would *you* like to do?" the child is encouraged to think creatively. Children spend so many hours in a structured environment at school, what a blessing for them to lead the way. The more often you listen to your child and show him that you value his ideas, the more you contribute to his self-esteem. What better time than playtime to give your children's imaginations free rein. It can lead them — and you — to wonderful places.

When children have good ideas and you follow through on them, they become confident in their ability to make decisions. My daughters always decided what game to play, and I fully and enthusiastically participated in their choices. When we played house, they picked and planned out the scenarios, many of which I still remember as quite amazing.

> *There was language in their very gesture.*
>
> *— William Shakespeare*

My children often directed us to museums. When Alexandra was eight and wanted to go to the Frick Museum, we were told that she had to be ten before being admitted to see the collection. Instead of waiting two years, I wrote a letter to the curator of the museum pleading Alexandra's case. We were soon invited to wander throughout the museum, fulfilling Alexandra's wishes.

As soon as they could talk, Alexandra and Brooke helped plan their own birthday parties. Celebrating your children's birthdays is a joyful way of honoring the importance of their lives. Birthdays are especially important in our family. When it came time to plan birthday parties, I turned to the girls for all the creative decision-making. We'd choose the invitations together, select the stamps. Every detail was the result of everyone's input. We decorated the apartment, cooked and baked together. They learned the whole process of having friends over to celebrate. Preparations and arrangements would go on for months before the actual date.

If my heart can become pure and simple like that of a child, I think there probably can be no greater happiness than this.

— Kitaro Nishida

Alexandra and Brooke's parties were always colorful and imaginative. One year, we decided the tablecloths at Dennison's Party Store on Fifth Avenue weren't exactly what we had in mind. So we went to the paint store and bought a drop cloth and painted bold Matisse-like cutout shapes all over it with acrylic paints. We found plastic plates and cups in hot pink, yellow, acid green, and cobalt blue. On the bottom of each cup and plate we painted an abstract design, putting the initials of each friend in the middle. After the party, we washed the plates and cups and put the sets in the guests' party bags as keepsake favors.

In addition to creative eating at these birthday parties, we had treasure hunts, painted murals, and made Peter play Peter Rabbit in costume, at the girls' request. Peter wouldn't have missed this opportunity for the world. Aside from Peter and myself, no adults were ever invited to these parties.

We've had the pleasure of getting to know many of our daughters' friends over the years, from these birthday parties. We'd see new faces, and some of the old familiar ones would

Exploring nature with your child is largely a matter of becoming receptive to what lies around you.

— Rachel Carson

drop out, but there was always a sweet feeling of continuity. Now that the children are grown, often, after one of these gatherings, several friends who have come from a distance spend the night, often just grabbing a quilt from a stack in my bedroom and sleeping on the floor. It's like having a sleep-over. I've always loved to see the entire available floor space in the apartment taken up with warm bodies in sleeping bags.

Making Yourself Accessible to Children

When I was little, my godmother let me call her by her first name, Mitzi. It made me feel so grown up and special that today, I never ask anyone—young or old—to call me anything but Alexandra, except, of course, to the handful of old friends who call me Sandie. Some parents think their child is acting presumptuous by calling me Alexandra and they whisper in their child's ear "Mrs. Stoddard." But I immediately assure moms that I invited their children to call me Alexandra. In some ways, this sums up my feelings about how to enjoy our children. We have to enter into the world *with* them, not above them or against them.

Recently, a six-year-old girl in church pointed to me, and exclaimed, "There's my friend Alexandra." The child's mother looked all around for a child. "There's Alexandra, over there. She's wearing red stockings."

I was with some of my small friends recently when "Alexandra" became "Mrs. Stoddard," the result of an adult request. I teased one child, saying, "We're friends and I'm no different from you. We're playing together, having fun. You make me feel like a dreary old lady when you call me Mrs. Stoddard. I'm a child, just like you." She laughed, saying, "No, you're not a child, Alexandra, because you take care of children." Why not do both, I say.

Children always sense when you enjoy being with them. They know from the energy you display. When I am with any child, I like to think I play my part to spread light and emphasize all the good and beautiful things in life. When I'm playing with children, I completely lose my self-consciousness. I become lighthearted because I am simply open to experience.

Is there ever a meaningless excursion when you are playing with a child? Absolutely not. Enjoying children is always a great experience. Both you and your child break through time barriers to a transcendent moment of pure experience.

I love to skip and dance, play hopscotch and touch football. I'm aware of my body, but not my age, or what others might think of my behavior, because I can be so in tune with the joy of the moment. When you shed your *shoulds* and *musts*, you become clearheaded, fresh-spirited, washed with the holy water of grace rather than the muddy water of turmoil. These silly times full of make-believe, wonder, and fantasy are wonderful—and fleeting. They can't be contrived because like all joy, there is a touch of the divine in them. We can't nail down the ingredients that make for the best atmosphere for enjoying our children. We simply have to be open to play.

What feeling is so nice as a child's hand in yours? So small, so soft and warm, like a kitten huddling in the shelter of your clasp.

— Marjorie Holmes

If you obey all the rules you miss all the fun.

— Katharine Hepburn

Chapter 6

Letting Your Children Go

Your children are not your children.
They are the sons and daughters of
Life's longing for itself.
They come through you but not from you,
And though they are with you, yet they
belong not to you.

—Kahlil Gibran
The Prophet

Meeting the Challenge of Letting Go

As mothers, we are constantly in the process of letting go of our children. We are confronted with letting go from the first moments of life. We let go as our new-born baby is cut from our umbilical cord and we're anxious about how well she takes her first feeding. We let go as our infant learns to walk and we begin to worry about his falling. We let go the first day we bring our child to daycare and walk out the door without him, placing him in the care of others for now. And we let go as our child chooses friends, lovers, schools, and her future, sad that we are no longer the center of her universe. We are touched by every signal, every sign of change—new shoes, a new tooth, a new grade at school, new freedom. Being a mother will always be a little bittersweet because of this. It is sweet to feel proud of our children,

With a smile on her lips, and a tear in her eye.

— Sir Walter Scott

delighted with their healthy independence. And it is a little bitter to know that because of this independence our connection to them will change.

Letting go is also painful because we know that there are limits to what we can continue to do for our children. In each stage of our child's development we learn anew both the struggles and the satisfactions of letting go. It is one of the greatest challenges we mothers face. As my friend Carl would say, "This is the way it should be."

Letting Go a Little Every Day

I once read that a mother is a person to lean on but one who also makes leaning unnecessary. When we've really done our job well, inch by inch, moment by moment, because of our help, our children will need us less and less. Suddenly, our daughter doesn't want to spend so much time with us, preferring to be with friends. We walk our son to school every day, but one morning at breakfast he announces, "I'm walking to school with Sam." And adds, "Mom, don't worry. I'll look both ways." Our heart drops to the kitchen floor. We burn ourselves as we clumsily serve the scrambled eggs, trying to hide our tears. We think, *What, my little baby crossing the street without holding my hand?* Or when our daughters kiss us good-bye at the apartment door before the elevator opens—for fear they'll be seen kissing their mom—we die a little inside. Yes, we let go a little every day. We lengthen the invisible cord, and help expand the boundaries of our children's world. We also pray and worry a lot.

> Respect the child.
> Be not too much
> his parent.
> Trespass not on
> his solitude.
>
> — Emerson

Change is inevitable. To understand and accept this requires that we be patient with both ourselves and our children. We're all learning how to let go together. When my former husband moved from New York to Los Angeles, every summer, beginning when Alexandra was seven and Brooke was four, I'd take them to Kennedy Airport to board an American Airlines flight, nonstop to Los Angeles, unescorted. The stewardess would let me see them to their seats and help them fasten their seat belts. After that, I would leave them in her care. The first time I left them I had a lump in my throat and couldn't swallow for three days. My babies were flying away from their mommy for seven weeks. They had a wonderful time on that first motherless journey and that helped me to bear in mind this milestone in our relationship.

He who would love must first learn to run through snow leaving no footprint.

— Native American proverb

Whenever one of the girls would do anything for the first time—take her first steps, speak her first words, start school, sleep overnight at a friend's house—I'd feel a heaviness in my heart with the realization that she was growing up. Watching them crossing the street without me for the first time made my mind lurch ahead to the day when each would leave for college. All these turning points raise paradoxical feelings in us. We want them to grow up, and yet we can't bear to let them go.

I keep learning, though, over and over again, the lesson that change is good; one door closes and another one opens. As my daughters grew, so did our relationship. After a period of separation, whether one night or seven weeks, whenever I would pick up Alexandra or Brooke, they'd be so full of excitement and intimate stories that they wanted to share with me, that they would always make me laugh. I felt flushed with warmth and the realization that their growth was a good, natural, and mysterious part of some divine process.

When you watch your child at a dance class or see her in a school play, you suddenly become aware that she has a big, wide-open world ahead of her. And that is good. You see that she has many people to teach her and love her, people who by becoming friends and even family participate in nurturing her, and that opens you in some way to others, too. We mothers tend to nurture all the children we come into contact with. We enjoy being able to support these tender souls as they flower in their transformations. Just because our children have grown up doesn't mean our maternal feelings and generosity have left us. We can mother, we can use this gift with many others. The feeling stays with us forever.

The young on their way to maturity long for privacy, physical and spiritual.

— Phyllis McGinley

The evolution from infancy to becoming a young baby, to being a toddler, to adolescence and adulthood, is ephemeral, with each stage lasting for only a brief time. By living in the center of each growth period, the process of nurturing our child through each precious stage of development can be and should be the most natural thing in life. Weaning Alexandra and Brooke off breast milk was a mutual letting go. The girls objected at first, yet, gradually, they got used to the idea of drinking out of a bottle. For my part, I had trouble facing that the girls were no longer biologically dependent on me—and only me. Others could provide their necessary nutrition with store-bought milk and a plastic bottle.

When Peter and I went off to Paris on our honeymoon, the girls were ages seven and four. It was hard for the girls to let their mommy go, and equally hard for me to leave them. But at the same time, Peter and I wanted to begin our union with a romantic escape together, and the girls, though sad to see me go, were happy for us.

It's not the love that we let go of, but the dependence; the love continues. While we'll always be interdependent, as mothers we foster autonomy and change for our children. By accepting the natural law of change and transformation, we gain the wisdom that allows us to live happily.

As the Buddha says:

This existence of ours is as transient as
    autumn clouds.
To watch the birth and death of beings
    is like looking at the movements of a
    dance.
A lifetime is like a flash of lightning in
    the sky.
Rushing by like a torrent down a steep
    mountain.

The best way I know to let go is to do so with love in your heart. Because of that love, so generously given, your children will always have a place to return to. No matter what life throws them, they will know that your love will see them through. Your love expresses the faith you have in your child's ability to take care of herself, and she will be buoyed up by this.

Separate from my boundaries, I had known before that he had and would have a life beyond being my son....He was three and I was nineteen, and never again would I think of him as a beautiful appendage of myself.

— Maya Angelou

Helping Your Children Fly

The female American bald eagle builds her nest out of thorns covered with soft fuzzy feathers. When her eaglets are born and need comfort, they are nurtured by this environment. But as they develop, the layer of feathers wears thin and they begin to feel the prickling of the thorns. This is the mother's indication to her young—her push for them—to leave the nest and fly away. For human mothers, the indications are not so strikingly clear.

Sometimes our child acts as if she cannot live without us. This can make us want to hold on to her more, even though this may be an opportunity to help her along her own path toward self-reliance. Your six-month-old baby may cry when you put her down. You think, *If I just hold her everything will be OK—she needs me.* But soon you learn that perhaps she doesn't need you to hold her, but rather, she needs you to help her help herself by putting her down with a toy to play with instead. A mother is always in the process of distinguishing between taking care of her child and teaching her child to take care of herself.

> *It is better to bind your children to you by a feeling of respect, and by gentleness, than by fear.*
>
> *— Terence*

When the girls were very young and their father and I were separated, I let them sleep in my bed. While I don't regret this temporary switch in sleeping patterns, the time came when I felt they should sleep in their own beds, in their own rooms. Many parents have trouble enforcing this transition because their children are very persuasive. I have learned that one helpful way to smooth the transition is to let your child spend a few nights in a sleeping bag in your bedroom before making her return to her own bed for good.

We experience this letting-go process in all the different stages of our children's lives. We see toddlers confront and succeed at walking. No sooner have they mastered that challenge when another challenge takes its place. They will be frustrated. They will feel incompetent when they try but cannot draw a certain picture, or fail at putting a puzzle together, and give up. We are tempted to help them with the picture or do the puzzle for them. So, when we bite our lip, stop ourselves from turning the missing pieces of the puzzle right side up and putting them in their hands, we are recognizing that ultimately this is their challenge, not ours. We have to respect their learning process, not always worry about it.

You have delighted us long enough.

— Jane Austen

Sometimes you have to give your child a little nudge, as painful as it may be for both of you. The first day of school, your child may hold on to you for dear life, tears streaming, wanting desperately to go home with you. You know you must leave her with her new teacher. We expose our children to safe challenges and encourage healthy experimentation and risk-taking because we understand the thrill of accomplishment from our own life's adventure. Each accomplishment is another feather that decorates a child's hat, creating a feeling of pride and self-satisfaction. We are letting go

Perhaps we have been misguided into taking too much responsibility for our children, leaving them little room for discovery.

— Helen Hayes

To lead the people, walk behind them.

— Lao-tzu

There is nothing more thrilling in this world, I think, than having a child that is yours, and yet is mysteriously a stranger.

— Agatha Christie

intelligently. The fun is in their learning, conquering, overcoming a challenge and being able to stretch their curiosity. Left to their own resources, children will be inquisitive, and pry into everything because of an innate eagerness to learn.

Our job is to encourage, not to be judgmental. We are not meant to wrap our egos around our children's development and push them too far. Any time we become excessively anxious about our children's success, from toilet training to test scores, we interfere with their natural ability to feel good about life.

We must be vigilant in seeing the opportunities to help our children to let go. We will not always be there when our children wake up. We owe it to our children to help and encourage them to move away, to fly out on their own, gradually. Because without our help to do so, our children will not be able to survive on their own.

I've seen how some mothers refuse to acknowledge their responsibility to let their children fly on their own wings. One woman redecorated her son's bedroom for him long after he was out on his own. Strangely, her son has returned to live at home without having created a life of his own. I have also watched parents do their children's homework, and I've observed children being privately tutored without a school's knowledge.

Even the best mothers have trouble mediating the delicate balance between providing comfort and security and fostering independence. Some may feel that they have just grown close to their son or their daughter, just started taking pleasure in their maturing connection, when their children start getting ready to leave. Such parents feel there is some basic injustice being perpetrated on them. It is a loss to them and loss feels painful. It can also be confusing. It may even make some parents feel angry or abandoned.

You have to love your children unselfishly. That's hard. But it's the only way.

— Barbara Bush

But many of us are grateful for having healthy, well-rounded children who figure things out in their own time, without the fear of letting their parents down. If we allow our children to grow into who they are, they will fly on their own wings.

Dr. Stephen Emlen, whose background is ornithology, applies his theories to human families. In an article in *The New York Times*, writer Natalie Angier points out that Dr. Emlen came up with more birds suiting his definition of family than mammals. Angier writes, "A hallmark of human families is the persistent contact between generations, and the substantial influence that parents continue to have on their children." She adds that "the number of creatures that congregate in these sorts of extended family structures is very small, about 3 percent of all mammals and birds."

Where, oh where are the children...?

— Colette

When we help our children fly away, we shouldn't cling to their wings. We always want to maintain contact with our children, but the time comes when the need for our influence wanes.

When Children Become Grown-ups

The struggle to separate reaches a whole new level as children become young adults and begin to step out into the world themselves. Letting go at seventeen or eighteen becomes a fundamentally new challenge. Now your children can drive cars, take trips to far-away places on their own, have intimate encounters, and try on the role of burgeoning adult. This stage becomes a true test of our ability as mothers to respect the separateness, the dignity, and the right to privacy of our children.

The closed bedroom door to your son's room is less about shutting you out than it is about his need to establish and enclose his sense of self. Purple hair is less about a rejection of your sensibilities than it is about your teenager's search for her own. A mother who tries to change her teenage son's behavior will find that he will be even more guarded against her, because her interference makes him feel not only that he has a fragile hold on himself, but that he will never be allowed to be himself around her. The mother of a young woman I know was so exasperated by her daughter's blue hair that she told her to dye it back to black or she would not be allowed to return home. The girl ended up leaving home at seventeen. Though it was difficult for her to be thrown out on her own, she chose not to put up with her mother's threats, knowing it would be the first of many if she stayed. What an awful choice for a child to have to make. Is it really worth abandoning your child because she has a need to express something you don't understand? I don't think so. Ultimately, your children are

> The first of earthly blessings, independence
>
> — Edward Gibbon

going to do what they need to do. A parent cannot, and should not, have control over a child's life.

It is normal that a child will go to extremes to distinguish himself from parents; it is a basic step in the formation of a self. As mothers, we should always be there for our children as they face this challenge. That's the best way I know to insure their strength in this delicate transition.

We mothers may also exhibit a certain insensitivity when we offer unsolicited opinions to our children. As much as I adored my mother, she was often unfeeling as to the effect of her opinions on me. When I was a young adult, her advice sometimes had a sting to it. There were many times I felt like wandering around the house barefoot, blouse untucked and wrinkled. "Go to your room and don't come out until you're properly dressed" was not the response I needed at the time. Coming down the stairs, seeing her seated at the secretary desk in the front hall, I would have loved it if she had said, "Hi, darling Sandie. How are you?" and had put down her pen, removed her glasses, reached over to me and offered me a hug, asking, "What can I do for you?" Instead I was sent back to my room to tuck in my blouse.

I am always ready to learn, although I do not always like being taught.

— Winston Churchill

While a strict upbringing has some advantages, there are times when a child needs to be reassured that she is wonderful just as she is. When Alexandra was four, I learned she knew what she wanted to wear to school, and that was a wonderful Zen lesson for me to allow her wild expression without my judging it. When she picked out her purples, pinks, and yellows, plaids, stripes, and checks, she owned the day, her day.

Recently, I heard a friend tell her married daughter, "That lipstick looks terrible with your dress. It's too dark." Though a

You cannot teach a child to take care of himself unless you will let him try to take care of himself. He will make mistakes; and out of these mistakes will come him wisdom.

— Henry Ward Beecher

mother may feel that she is just "trying to help," her child would be helped more by her silent support and encouragement. When Alexandra and Brooke want my advice, they ask me. They're not shy about asking and are quick to decide whether my opinions will be useful or not.

As the Buddha so beautifully instructs, "To give your cow or sheep a large spacious meadow is the best way to control him."

In contrast, I love it when the girls offer me unsolicited advice: "Mom, it's time to retire the hot-pink lipstick. Let's pick one that's softer." Maybe I like it because all those years I focused my attention on them, and now, it feels good to be focused on by them.

I remember crossing this threshold myself one Friday night when Brooke was twenty-five. She borrowed my black shawl, and a few days later, it arrived from the dry cleaner. Why would a shawl need to be cleaned after one evening? I wondered. Maybe it smelled like cigarette smoke from a bar, or perhaps she had spilled something on it. "You don't want to know, Mom," Brooke replied when I inquired. She was right!

Think back to your own adolescence. Did your mother know when you had had too much to drink? Did she know the details of your romances? Did she talk to you about sex and other intimacies? Mine surely didn't. And I grew up just fine. If your daughter doesn't ask your advice on these matters, chances are your opinions are not needed. Recalling that, I have always worked especially hard to respect my daughters' privacy. While we had many meaningful and important discussions, I always tried to provide information without being intrusive. And it was not always easy, particularly since we had such a close relationship, and loved each other's company. Perhaps it's the space and respect I gave them that enabled us to be so close; they knew I would not cross the line. They knew that I was open to their lives as independent beings. Alexandra and Brooke brought home boyfriends whom I wasn't exactly crazy about, but I accepted that they were free to make their own choices. I understood that if they were to learn what they needed to learn about life, they would have to do it in their own time, in their own way. It wasn't always easy. I had to work on myself not to get too involved.

In case of doubt, it is better to say too little than too much.

— Thomas Jefferson

I tried to stay available without interfering. There is a natural tendency on a mother's part to have opinions about nearly everything concerning her children. I learned to trust Alexandra and Brooke's judgment and put my faith in them.

When a mother fails to allow her children that space for themselves—a place where they can be who they are—their love backfires. It's then that many children deliberately put real space between themselves and their parents by moving away.

Just a few years ago, I teased my brother Powell for moving to Chicago many years ago to put some distance between himself and my mother. He argued, "No, Sandie, I was relocated by my work." Powell then gave me a little wink. Powell and my mother were very close. But sometimes in such a close mother-son relationship, distance becomes useful, sometimes necessary.

Children know how to get the space they need. When

Brooke went to live in Paris after she graduated from college, she defined her own life, her own interests, and her own passions. They were different from her family's. But we knew that was a very good thing. When your child goes off to explore the world alone, though it may sometimes keep you awake at night, the knowledge that she is learning about life and how to be a strong participant in it can make you feel very proud indeed. It shows you what a good job you've done. She can now fly on her own energy.

Letting Go of Financial Support

I think it's important to offer a few thoughts on the sensitive issue of financial support—how much, how little—which is a key consideration when letting our children grow into independent adults.

Can a woman forget her sucking child, that she should not have compassion on the son of her womb?

— Isaiah

In our continuing efforts to aid our children's inner growth, their spiritual and physical unfolding, how does money come into play? If you have the means, it's wonderful to give your newly independent child money to take a trip with a friend or buy an important item, say, a computer. Indeed, it's a generous and loving act. And helping your child to get settled after college or in a first job also helps to facilitate his or her growth. Unfortunately, given our current economy and with the job prospects being as abysmal for young people as they are, we might be called upon to help for a longer period than is good. Some things are out of our hands, and we must appreciate those facts. But the sooner your children experience themselves as financially independent beings, the sooner they will feel faith and pride in themselves. I left home when I was sixteen and never went back to be dependent on family. Whenever I did go home, I went back as an independent adult, which was very important to me.

Some parents may continue to support a child well beyond a reasonable time in order to keep a connection through dependence. Other parents even go so far as to feel that giving money justifies meddling in their child's affairs. I know of one mother whose daughter became a painter, and at one of her shows, the mother explained that these were "her" own paintings because she made it possible for her daughter to work. This, of course, is an extreme case, but it nevertheless reflects the dangerous manipulative power that money can have in a family.

Supporting sons and daughters financially when they need help getting back on their feet or extra money to carry them through an especially hard time is a gift of love, even if the money is a loan. There cannot be emotional strings attached. A loving parent uses money as a tool to help a child through some rough patches or to provide for educational opportunities. One of the nicest uses of money is to give a small gift unexpectedly to a child. Whenever I've done this, Alexandra and Brooke usually thank me by saying, "How did you know?" Who couldn't use a small windfall every once in a while? I can't figure out who is happier under those circumstances, the giver or the receiver. I suspect it is quite equal.

> *Seeing you sleeping on your back among your stuffed ducks, bears and basset hounds would remind me that no matter how good the next day might be, certain moments were gone forever....*
>
> *— Joan Baez*

Being Open to Other Points of View

"Let yourself be open and life will be easier. A spoon of salt in a glass of water makes the water undrinkable. A spoon of salt in a lake is almost unnoticed." I find these words of the Buddha liberating. When we open our minds and listen to our children we may hear things we've never heard before. And even if they do not serve us in our own lives, what a thrill it is to know that our children are busy working life out for themselves.

Only in growth, reform and change, paradoxically enough, is true security to be found.

— Anne Morrow Lindbergh

When you trust in the processes that build emotional and spiritual growth, you can trust that your child will grow and develop into a strong, moral, happy, and compassionate person. All you will ever need to understand about letting your child go is in your heart, your mind, and your soul. If you look there, you will find that you understand your children's need to develop in their own way, in their own direction.

A mother who offers encouragement, support, and praise is doing precious work in nurturing a wonderful human being. If she recognizes the talents, the generosity, the honesty, and the right of her child to hold differing opinions, she adds immeasurably to that child's self-confidence. If she's tolerant, comforting, and trusting, her humanity will make letting go a graceful process.

Sometimes, we have to give up our prejudices to let our children be who they are. We have to stop finding fault, stop being so critical. We are not assigned to make them over. Self-improvement takes place inside each human soul; it is not transferred from our point of view to our children's. At times, our opinions can be hopelessly narrow and limited compared with how much wisdom our children may acquire at different stages of their growth. They are learning new things about the world, things that were not true for us when we were their age. Therefore, we must listen to them where they live.

We must understand that in many ways, today's world is much more challenging for young adults. There's a lot more cynicism and widespread pessimism about what the future holds. Young adults see their elders as more motivated by selfishness and greed than morality and optimism. I was born during World War II, raised to feel proud to be an American, glad to have freedom and democracy. We looked up to our political leaders as moral human beings. We had heroes, men and women noted for their nobility of purpose, and we celebrated their courage.

Today, our children also face a tougher job market. With businesses downsizing, relying more on technology than people, a good education doesn't necessarily open the doors of opportunity as it did decades ago. The world seems more spiritually bankrupt as moral conventions come crashing down.

The predominant mood of my growing-up years was upbeat and optimistic. We were all genuinely looking forward to the future with all its challenges and exciting adventures. Today, our children have to search harder than we did. We need to

> *If there is anything that we wish to change in the child, we should first examine it and see whether it is not something that could better be changed in ourselves.*
>
> *— Carl Jung*

stay conscious of this. When we do apply the wisdom of the Buddha to our children and let ourselves "be open," we will have an increased tolerance, a capacity to respect their beliefs and lifestyles, even when they are very different from our own. In each generation, every individual seeks the meaning of his or her world, finding what is true and good in each person's eyes and heart. By opening up to this authenticity, we actually encourage the growth of our children as they journey in the direction of personal truth and individual honesty.

> I like a little rebellion now and then. It is like a storm in the atmosphere.
>
> — Thomas Jefferson

It's healthy for mothers and their children to disagree. There's no reason to have a falling-out just because you have different views. Your children's views on politics, religion, clothes, or social behavior should not be seen as challenges to your own. At different stages in their development, children will argue with you just to distinguish themselves from you. This is a function of an emotional process built into human nature. You can become engaged with them in these disputes—you should, in fact take them seriously. But never, never take it personally and lash out.

> A youth is to be regarded with respect. How do you know that his future will not be equal to our present?
>
> — Confucius

I'm happy that no one I know is alienated from me because we disagree about politics, religion, cultural tastes, or lifestyle. One of the most hurtful disagreements I had with my own mother was over religious practice. Mother was raised a Roman Catholic and later joined the Episcopal Church, the faith in which she brought up her children. But when I left home at sixteen and traveled to the Far East, where I worshipped in Hindu and Buddhist temples and in tea ceremonies, then in European cathedrals and through my own quiet meditation, I grew to question much of what I'd been taught.

Mother had little tolerance for my doubts. Her faith grew from her own traditions, which were different from my own. One day, we were driving to Massachusetts to go a friend's funeral. "Sandie, dear," my mother began, "I don't understand how you can live without faith." I was shocked. At thirty-five, I felt I had a great deal of faith, more than I had ever had in my life. Nervously, I laughed. "Mother, I have faith. But you can't see it, touch it, taste it, smell it, or hear it. Believe me, my faith is not your problem. I'll continue to spend my life increasing my faith."

There is no trust unless you let go of yourself.

— Pope John XXIII

I don't think children can inherit a meaningful religion. I believe each one of us must challenge and doubt in order to find a spiritual practice that feels right to us. We should be glad to see our children exploring other faiths, traditions, beliefs, and practices. Only through such questioning can they come to know their own beliefs. My own growing sense of spirituality began in the Episcopal Church, of which I am still a member. I deeply appreciate all those years of instruction, guidance, and counseling, and the rituals, the music, fellowship, and sense of tradition. Church continues to be a comforting peaceful place for me. But I will never accept everything about any religion 100 percent. I've had to think for myself, unlearn some things, learn others, and deepen my personal experience of divinity in everyday living. I hope for no less from my children, if that is their wish.

go of. They've made the switch from turning to me for advice to confiding in each other a less difficult and awkward transition for me.

Once our children are adults, we should no longer have any continuing control over them. We can't hover, fluttering around as a presence suspended in space. We've been given our time to be with them; now, we're called upon to back off, let them have more of their own personal center of energy, without feeling suppressed, manipulated, or guilty.

Create a vital space that encourages your child's growth, creativity, curiosity, independence, and industry.

We can let our children move on to make their own mistakes—and to score their own victories. We have the ability to do so within ourselves, even though at times, their independence frightens us and we worry that we have lost a crucial role in life. We have our instincts and our intuition. And if we examine those very closely, very honestly, we will see that we have taught our children what they need to know to get started. The follow-through is up to them. They are going to make mistakes, mistakes that will cause them pain. But since we trust that we've taught them that they have all the tools within themselves to solve their problems, they will be OK. If they need us, we're there.

As our children leave home to start their own lives, and perhaps families, though we still may be central to their lives, we are no longer the center. And that is a new life passage for us to face. It doesn't happen all at once. We've had some practice over the years in watching our children grow into their inevitable independence. We can share the sadness and joy that tinge this loss with our children by sharing memories.

Childhood is something we are all giving up, and there is some comfort in going through that realization together.

In order to be prepared to let go of our children, we have to be whole ourselves. I love Alexandra and Brooke too much to be a dreary, sour, grumpy person. But I also love myself enough to know I deserve to be happy. We have to discover what we want to do now that we have a greater measure of freedom and the maturity to understand what suits our needs. This basic stability, this knowledge that life is good and we can always participate in its magnificent banquet, puts a mother in a far better position to let her children go. I've learned one of the most powerful ways to express my love for my children is to take good care of myself. So often, young adults feel sorry for the mother they abandoned as they look to their future so full of hope and high expectations.

We have an advantage now that we've raised our children. We've made a greater commitment to life, and now we know what's important to us and what it takes to get it. We've learned about patience, about struggle, about trying to be in control of everything, and about the virtues of taking risks. We've learned to manage on little sleep; we've trained ourselves to do several things at once, accumulating wisdom through experience. Having raised children, we understand that parenting continues forever, though in different forms. We continue to recognize that as we love our children, now as emancipated individuals—we can carry on where we left off with our separate lives. I have no doubts about it; this transition is an opportunity for both mother and child to grow and mature.

> *Children as a rule do not want to be indulged; they want to be responsible.*
>
> *— Hannah Lees*

We hear so much about midlife crises and empty-nest syndrome. But I see this passage as an opportunity for new relationships with our children, ourselves, and the world. It's ironic that my spiritual growth, which so horrified my mother and was the source of so much pain and anger between us, has allowed me to let go of Alexandra and Brooke with a sense of joy, rather than sadness.

All for love, and nothing for reward.

— Edmund Spenser

This constant inner growth, which I have worked on all my life, has enabled me to meet life's transitions with a sense of anticipation of still more growth. My journey in faith has always been all mine, and began long before I had children. A mother must take care to bolster her core identity during her mothering years. Not only does she benefit from taking charge and not letting her life be crowded out by other's needs, but she must find a way to develop her own personal passions and direction.

We recently celebrated Peter's birthday by spending the day with his daughter Andrée and her five-year-old son, James, who live in New York City. I was moved by Andrée's pursuits as a painter while being a mother of a young child. Andrée is aware that James won't stay so close to her forever; he'll be going off to school soon, so she'll have more time for herself. She's renting a studio with several friends she met at the Rhode Island School of Design, and is working toward having a solo show in a few years.

Marriage and After

After the children leave, not all mothers are in the same situation they were in when their children were born. Some women have lost their husbands through death or divorce. And not every mother who finds herself still married is happy with her life. Not everyone has a great marriage. In fact, many women stay in a bad relationship for their children's sake. But this may not have been as wise a strategy as they once thought. Studies have shown that children are healthier and happier when parents split up amicably than when they sacrifice their own happiness for their children's benefit. In such a situation, once the children are out of the home, the parents must face the emptiness of their marriage. If a mother does make this mistake, she may hold a grudge against her children, feeling they aren't grateful enough after all she has sacrificed for them.

Give birth to them and nourish them. Give birth to them but don't try to own them. Help them to grow but don't rule them. This is called Profound Virtue.

— Lao-tzu

Unfortunately, this is not uncommon. Divorces often occur after the youngest child leaves home and spouses come face-to-face with the realization that they no longer have strong feelings for each other. Often a mother will unknowingly place blame on her children for her empty marriage, associating their leaving the nest with her "sudden" failed marriage.

Children are not substitutes for spouses. A woman has the capacity to maintain a loving relationship with the man she married and still be a good nurturing mother after children are born. So many factors are involved. Just as the best way never to get fat is never to get fat, ideally, a man and a woman should never let anything interfere with their love for each other. Children can be difficult, often trying to pry a partnership apart. A mother puts her child first, but it should not be at the expense of her love for her spouse. It's not healthy for parents to be manipulated by a child. The great gift two loving parents

No matter how old a mother is, she watches her middle-aged children for signs of improvement.

— Florida Scott-Maxwell

can give their child is an example of just how happy mature love can be, and how strongly woven two people can become, inseparably giving whenever needed and sharing a good life together.

After the children leave home is the time to be proud of your accomplishments as a mother. You will continue to be rewarded throughout your life. When Peter and I dropped Brooke off at college in Granville, Ohio, we hopped back on the plane, held hands, and I inquired, "Where are we going for dinner, darling?" After cooking for twenty years, I felt it was time to be served. We acted our children's age, having the freedom not to be accountable. Children come first, but when they are no longer in the center of your daily life, your inner resources, your passions, and expanded love of life give your children confidence in their own ability to seek and find joy on their own individual paths.

Expanding Our Possibilities

When our children leave, we begin to do more things for ourselves. Some mothers feel a bit wobbly at first. But you'll soon get your sea legs and make deliberate efforts to learn, to stretch, to expand your heart and mind.

I also think we all have a divine urge, a need to express faith and lead a spiritual life—in whatever form it takes. You may fulfill this through your chosen faith, or find spiritual satisfaction in art, literature, meditation, or community work. Our higher self is always there just smiling at us, waiting for us to wake up. As mothers, it's important that we know that after so much giving of ourselves, we have a deeper, more enlightened place we can to return to.

For the working mother, the adjustment to our children leaving home is less dramatic. My career as an interior designer was, in some ways, an anchor for me. It was another source of strength and support. I always worked while my children were home, so I wasn't faced with the challenge of starting a new career. Many women do go back to part-time work or even full-time work while their children are still at home. It gives them a foot in the door, which helps future career planning. But even if you were at home full-time, the skills you learned and the wisdom of your experience as a mother will serve you well in many places in the working world. Don't underestimate this fact—even if others might! You have learned how to get things done, how to negotiate, how to strategize, how to solve numerous kinds of problems. You've put in plenty of overtime, stretched yourself physically, enlarged your mind, and learned to stand firm in the face of rebellion.

At the women's conference in China in 1995, the Nobel Peace Laureate from Myanmar, Daw Aung San Suu Kyi, delivered a message that should be heard loudly and clearly:

For millennia women have dedicated themselves almost exclusively to the task of nurturing, protecting, and caring for the young and the old, striving for the conditions of peace that favor life as a whole.

Style, in writing or speaking, is formed very early in life, while the imagination is warm and impressions are permanent.

— Thomas Jefferson

In one's family, respect and listening are the source of harmony.

— Buddha

Also, take a look back at some of the passions or interests you may have cultivated. Perhaps you would still like to spend more time with children? You could look into work in family planning or as a child advocate. You might work in a daycare center or a family-child crisis agency. Consider becoming a teacher or tutor, a child psychologist, camp counselor, a pediatric nurse or doctor, which of course means going back to school. Or you might study child development. There are activities that don't require formal training; my editor's mother, at age seventy, volunteers at a local hospital, rocking premature babies.

You know children are growing up when they start asking questions that have answers.

— John J. Plomp

You don't have to sign up for an "official" role to stay in touch with children and your maternal essence. You can baby-sit for a young family as a favor so the parents can go out on the town for an evening's romance. Or, you can invite children over for a tea party and to do art projects. Our skills as nurturers can be put to good use in a broad range of disciplines. A great way to engage children is to bring them into your world. An artist friend felt like making a huge mural of the harbor in Martha's Vineyard. Brenda, as Michelangelo before her, needed helpers. She went around to her neighbors and succeeded in gathering a dozen children of various ages. The group trooped down to the harbor, and, once there, Brenda attached an entire roll of white shelf paper to a fence so these blossoming artists could paint what they saw. After ice-cream cones and cookies, she invited all the

I take up a lot of space.

— Brooke Stoddard

children's parents over for iced tea and to see the creation, which she displayed by hanging a ribbon across two trees and attaching the mural to it with clothespins. The afternoon shadows were deep against brilliant sunshine, setting these pure, intense colors on fire with energy and inner light as the mural shimmered and danced in the crisp breeze.

Whether you decide to launch a new career or become more involved in community work, this can be one of the richest and most rewarding periods of your life. One woman I know gradually became more involved in the arts in her town and is now on the city council planning to run for her state's House of Representatives. Another woman I met while on one of my book tours went to law school at the age of forty, and now works as an assistant district attorney in the town were she lives and raised her children. I know women who work in fund-raising at institutions dedicated to passionate causes. After raising four children and painting part time, another friend committed herself to being a full-time artist, and her paintings are now in great demand.

When our responsibilities to our children shift into low gear, we must remember how competent we are, how much mothering has taught us. We're well qualified to perform many acts, suitable to our own current interests which are honed over a lifetime. After my friend Mary Ann's two daughters left Jackson, Mississippi, to go to college out of state, although her formal education was in psychology, she began to use her innate decorating skills to help friends with their homes. She

> *Where love is present, where parents put each other first, children look forward to coming home; they feel like counting the hours.*
>
> *— Eknath Easwaran*

> *Oppose a negative wave of thought with a positive wave of thought.*
>
> — *Buddha*

loves being paid for her talent. But she also runs seminars and conferences on a volunteer basis to benefit her community.

I myself have so enjoyed the greater time I've had to read since my grown daughters left home. I have a huge collection of books that I regularly dive into as a constant source of inspiration and enlightenment. I'd like to share my list of favorites with you:

Madeleine L'Engle, *A Circle of Quiet*
C. S. Lewis, *Surprised by Joy; The Four Loves; A Grief Observed*
Rainer Maria Rilke, *Letters to a Young Poet*
Pierre Teilhard de Chardin, *The Phenomenon of Man; The Divine Milieu*
John B. Coburn, *A Diary of Prayers; Grace in All Things; The Hope of Glory; Anne and the Sand Dobbies; Feeding Fire*
Kahlil Gibran, *The Prophet; A Tear and a Smile*
Meister Eckehart, *Selected Writings*
Saint Augustine, *The Confessions of Saint Augustine*
Paul Tillich, *The New Being*
Blaise Pascal, *Pensées*
Rollo May, *The Discovery of Being; Love and Will; The Courage to Create; Freedom and Destiny; My Quest for Beauty; Existential Psychology*
Gerald May, *Will and Spirit; Care of Mind/Care of Spirit*
Dietrich Bonhoeffer, *Act of Being*
René Dubos, *A God Within; Beast or Angel; Choices That Make Us Human; Celebrations of Life; So Human an Animal*
Dag Hammarskjöld, *Markings*
Michael Drury, *Advice to a Young Wife from an Old Mistress*

Nikos Kazantzakis, *Zorba the Greek; Report to Greco*
Emily Dickinson, *Collected Poems of Emily Dickinson*
Ralph Waldo Emerson, *Selected Essays*
Eric Butterworth, *The Concentric Perspective (What's in It for Me)*
Plato, *Republic; Symposium*
Lin Yutang, *The Importance of Living; The Gay Genius; The Best of an Old Friend; My Country and My People; Looking Beyond*
Norman Vincent Peale, *The Power of Positive Thinking*
Søren Kierkegaard, *Either/Or*
Dame Julian of Norwich, *Selected Writings*
Johann Wolfgang von Goethe, *Theory of Colours*
Alan Watts, *The Way of Zen*
Albert Schweitzer, *Selected Writings*
Lao-tzu, *Tao Te Ching; The Canon of Reason and Virtue*
Michel de Montaigne, *Essays and Selected Writings*
Confucius, *The Wisdom of Confucius; The Analects*
Sophocles, *The Oedipus Cycle*
Erich Fromm, *The Art of Loving; Escape from Freedom; Man for Himself*
The Buddha, *Selected Writings*
Anne Morrow Lindbergh, *Gift from the Sea; Hour of Gold, Hour of Lead*
Eknath Easwaran, *Words to Live By; Conquest of Mind*
Joseph Campbell, *The Power of Myth*
Antoine de Saint-Exupéry, *The Little Prince*
Carl Jung, *The Undiscovered Self; Memories, Dreams, Reflections; Psychological Reflections*
William James, *The Varieties of Religious Experience*
George Santayana, *The Sense of Beauty*

Aristotle, *Ethics*
Sogyal Rinpoche, *Tibetan Book of Living and Dying*
Jacques Barzun, *A Stroll with William James*
Virginia Woolf, *A Room of One's Own*

From Mother to Lover to Fabulous Companion

Immortality is won by acquiring the wisdom of acceptance, taking what comes along, for in going along with things, an individual avoids becoming separated from them.

— Greta K. Nagel

A love life? How long has it been since you've thought of having a love life? Maybe very long. But not *that* long, nor is it forgotten. You're still full of energy and sexuality. So what is your relationship with your husband like now? Have you remained intimately connected? If you and your husband were industrious and kept your love life alive at any available time during the raising of your children, bravo! If you haven't, well, here's your chance.

When our children were all out of the house, Peter and I took little island vacations like young lovers, making me freshly aware of how attractive I still was to him and he to me. We'd go on a trip to an inn on a lake or skiing to escape all the distractions of our daily life at home. We'd pretend we were newlyweds, holding hands, hugging, and staring into each other's eyes. When you're home, create a loving, warm atmosphere, conducive to intimacy. Candlelight, classical music, and wine or sparkling mineral water sipped out of cut-crystal stemmed glasses after a productive but frantic day can soothe you into tenderness and touching.

Husbands can be of great help and support during this transition. Peter and I began to have a lot more fun together and to be better companions and friends after my daughters were on their own. Just as you did many activities with your children, you can take classes with your spouse, go horseback riding, or study ceramics together. I know a couple in Denver who took up rock climbing when their last child left for college.

You're still a family, and as you now love your children from a distance, you can adjust your priorities and spend more time together as wife and husband. Mothers of grown children have a wealth of love to give. This energy seeks a wide variety of channels, and the richness of our mature years depends on our directing this powerful force in ever-deepening ways.

Soul-making is a journey that takes time, effort, skill, knowledge, inspiration, and courage.

– Thomas Moore

I believe a mother's love for her children makes her a more magnificent lover to her spouse; the flow of unqualified love flows to her partner. We've learned so much along our paths. We tend not to judge, but try to understand. Just as we let our children be our teachers, now that the noise and hectic schedules have died down, we can take time to pay attention to the wisdom and grace our husbands or companions are waiting to share with us, undividedly. Just as a mother is always a mother, she is always a woman who, when there's someone to love, she's there, loving.

When we raise children, they are right in front of our noses. They're immediate, here and now, and we live with them at close range. A mother is given this privilege, this divine gift, becoming enlightened in her own backyard, at the kitchen table, on the floor of the nursery. When a child leaves home, the illumination of consciousness doesn't go away; the light sparkles as the sun on the water, because we've discovered the secret of life. The true way to find contentment is at home, with your loved ones, all of them, as though they are stars piercing through darkness.

Let us not be weary in well-doing: for in due season we shall reap.

— Galatians

Being a mother has amplified my ability to love beauty, to love all the goodness in our midst, but it has especially taught me to appreciate the little gestures, the kindness of my spouse, the caring, the thoughtfulness, and the sweetness of daily life at home. We had a friend who told Peter and me we spend too much time together. Peter's answer amused me. "Alan, Alexandra and I came together late in life. We're just making up for lost time and loving every minute."

When we began living without the children under our roof, Peter was no longer just there as a loving presence. He became my date, my entertainment, and my muse. We ritualized our evenings together, making plans, deciding what we wanted to do, when we wanted to dine, where we'd sit to relax and review the day's events. Everything was different because we were alone. Because we joined each other after we had children and previous marriages, we'd never spent much time alone together. This time for us was extremely happy, and continues to be. We seem to grow on each other the more we share in life's riches.

Peter's support during this transition was immeasurable. He encouraged me to go on more book tours, coming along whenever he could. We travel together more now that we have flexibility with our work and no domestic obligations.

We made a few adjustments to the rhythm of our days when Brooke went to college. She left on a Sunday and on Monday, we worked late at our respective offices. Afterward we went to a local bistro for supper and then to a movie. Going home for dinner without a child there seemed sad, almost like a little death. All those years racing home early to be there for Alexandra and Brooke and then just for Brooke were over. We no longer had to call to check in during the day. No one was home. But we were free to do whatever we wanted. Ironically, we felt like children again—with no parents to watch over us! Peter and I accepted our situation as inevitable. It was time for the children to move on, and we felt we were sprung free, rising to a new chapter with fresh challenges. The mother was on her way to a new, exciting transition.

There is always one moment in childhood when the door opens and lets the future in.

— Graham Greene

When Kahlil Gibran speaks about raising and letting go of children, his wisdom rings true:

You are the bow from which your children as
living arrows are sent forth.
Let your bending in the archer's hand be for
gladness;
For even as he loves the arrow that flies, so
He loves also the bow that is stable.

Chapter 7

Grandmothers and Other Significant Women in Our Lives

Nothing is so strong as gentleness,
nothing so gentle as real strength.

—St. Francis de Sales

The Many Mothers in Our Lives

There's an old expression that says, "It takes an entire village to raise one child." No doubt, as a mother, you're nodding your head in agreement. It takes enormous energy and attention to raise a child; it's remarkable that any mother thinks she can do it all with only the help of her partner. It's hard work. That's why so many people come to play an important role in a child's life. I cannot imagine having raised Alexandra and Brooke without the wisdom and support of my mother, my friends, and all my women mentors.

A mother's influence is broad, profound, and permanent, but she is not our only female

> Becoming a grandparent is a second chance, for you have a chance to put to use all the things you learned the first time....It's all love and no discipline.
>
> — Dr. Joyce Brothers

> *Wisdom is a special knowledge in excess of all that is known.*
>
> — Ambrose Bierce

provider of maternal love and support. Grandmothers, aunts, godmothers, mothers-in-law, step-mothers, teachers, and some of our friends can be the most energetic and generously engaged nurturers. Other women can become so important that often, when we think about it, we cannot imagine life without their help. We may go to our own experienced mother for advice. We often ask our mother friends for a reality check when we feel pushed to the limit — "Is this normal," we ask? We go to teachers and mentors to take a page from their books on raising children. We may turn to an aunt for her sense of balance. When raising a child, it is both inevitable and life affirming to turn to a wide community of experienced mothers. We turn to them not only for their parenting advice, but because of our own need for support and reassurance that, no matter what, we will survive to see our children thrive.

Grandmothers Are Grand

My mother was transformed when she became Alexandra and Brooke's grandmother. She became a different person when she graduated into the magic realm of grandmotherdom, where she reigned as both healer and cheerleader. She threw out all the rule books and suspended judgment and impatience; curbing and altering her grandchildren's behavior was not her everyday duty — as it is with mothers. There were no strings attached to her love. Mother could finally be the fairy "grand" mother and give her pure, basic, unconditional love.

Miraculously, Mother shed all the weighty emotional baggage she had carried over a lifetime of difficulties. During her own childhood, she had had a heart murmur that deprived her of a formal education. Then she had suffered greatly during her mothering years, and sometimes it showed. Besides the normal struggles of raising four children, she had been brokenhearted by an unfaithful husband. So life was sometimes hard for her, and among other more substantial deprivations, there was little money for travel, a passion that was central to her life. Such constraints made her difficult to live with at times; she could be critical and impatient with her children.

By the time Alexandra was born, Mother had been diagnosed with leukemia. Although the disease was largely in remission, she lived her days with a greater sense of urgency and intensity. Paradoxically, her loss of energy invigorated her to live as fully as she could, however she could, as long and as well as she could. With Alexandra and Brooke, Mother's spirit changed not only because of her new understanding of life's preciousness, but because the girls filled her with love. My tough, opinionated, and independent mother became a soft, warm, and wise woman. She showed her affection unabashedly for all her grandchildren. When the girls were young, Mother lived in a charming house which she affectionately called "The Studio," located on a pond beside a river in Westport, Connecticut.

A constant influence, a peculiar grace

— William Wordsworth

Experience is what really happens to you in the long run; the truth that finally overtakes you.

— Katherine Anne Porter

Of all the houses Mother turned into her home, this was obviously her favorite. The office for her business, Country Design Interiors, was located on the river a few blocks away. She had finally found where and how she wanted to live.

Secret gardens of the heart where the old stay young forever

— Judy Collins

Sharing time with Alexandra and Brooke made her radiate with joy. She would spend weekends with them alone. One autumn afternoon, I heard howls of laughter coming from Mother's house when I arrived on Sunday to pick up the girls. Mother was hiding the girls in mounds of yellow, saffron-colored, and orange maple leaves. They'd be very still and then break open from the high mound, screaming, "Peek-a-boo!" I must have watched this game for twenty minutes before I was noticed. The three girls were in the flow, out of body, unaware of time. Not only was I overjoyed to experience this exhilaration of loving energy, but I especially enjoyed the continuity. The mother who would temporarily abandon her cares to be fully present with me when I was a little girl, who excited me with her vitality and enthusiasm for life, was now reawakened to this spirit with the girls. That Indian summer afternoon, dressed in her jodhpurs and shiny, but now dusty black high riding boots, she was a living portrait of a great lady. Her vulnerability became her strength.

I have taken all knowledge to be my province.

— Francis Bacon

She was devoted to Alexandra and Brooke, and her heart opened to them in extraordinary ways. Of all her six grandchildren, our daughters lived the closest to her and were the most available. When they visited her, they went everywhere she went, as Mother showed them off to neighbors and clients. She took them out to her favorite restaurants, treating them like princesses. She was infinitely patient and adopted a Zen-like calm as she took the lead from Alexandra or Brooke. Mother adored Alexandra's crazy outfits of purple and pink, praised both girls' artistic talents as though each painting they did were a Matisse or a Picasso. Because they were "artists in the studio," she let them be messy. Canvas drop cloths were spread out on the living room floor where projects abounded. Nothing had a beginning or an end; there was only the moment. When it was time for the girls to leave, unfinished crafts and artwork were put away in a supply closet to await their next visit.

This *grand*mother congratulated the girls on everything they did, big and small. While Mother was a lady of style and sophistication, her prize objects were the girls' paintings and sculptures. She almost lost her mind when a friend used Brooke's red-clay hand imprint as an ashtray. Along with her art collection were framed drawings and pictures the girls had created in "The Studio," and I believe they were her most treasured objects of beauty.

Mother clearly was a latent artist who lived a conventional life until her divorce, when she came into her own as a creative women. She had come from an extremely artistic family. When she was with the girls, and I'm certain the same held true for her other grandchildren, she lived deeply in the present, doing everything on the spur of the

> *My mother was always there for us to offer her unconditional love and support at all times, which has taught me to become the special mother I believe I am. The art of mothering is handed down from one generation to the next. Thanks, Mom!*
>
> *— Wendy Jean Ruhl*

moment. Peter Pan–like, she could fly from storytelling to painting to dressing up. With her spirit present, there was always a sense of adventure and exhilaration. The girls loved her sense of pageantry. Even Saturday breakfast was a big event, where the waffle iron was center stage on the kitchen counter, jars of jam and honey were opened, and a tin shaker of confectioner's sugar stood ready for bizarre concoctions as well as a white clouding in the air.

Silver yields to gold, gold to virtue.

– Horace

As a grandmother, my mother metamorphosed from a gray moth into a radiant butterfly made brilliant by her love. I think Mother changed partly because she came to see her own losses as painful, and she realized that they had taught her something essential about life. My daughters benefited from my mother's hard-earned wisdom, and adored her for her love and generosity. In the words of my friend Jenni Fair, "They were her grands."

To me, faith means not worrying.

– John Dewey

Three of my mother's four children married and had children. At the time mother died, she had close, affectionate, and extremely meaningful relationships with six grandchildren: my older brother Powell's three children, Rob, Doug, and Laura; my two, Alexandra and Brooke; and my sister Barbara's son, Jamie.

Grandmothering allowed my mother the freedom to get back in touch with and share her childlike qualities. A grandmother can lift a child in her arms or plop down on the floor, grandchild planted in her lap. Becoming a grandmother renews a woman's sense of possibility. She feels a new connection to life. A grandmother is simply rejuvenated by her grandchildren. She becomes one of their favorite playmates. In truth, a grandmother can never be old when she is with her grandchildren.

Practically speaking, grandmothers no longer have to scramble, racing around all day to take care of all the household chores. Grandmothers can be cool, calm, and collected. Grandmothers are able to radiate nonjudgmental love that sometimes mothers cannot. Mothers are under a strain that grandmothers are not under. They can relax. A spilled plate of food no longer sends them into a tizzy; it doesn't happen every day, and it's not their problem. Now she's ready with a twinkle in her eye, and a nostalgic, fun story to tell. Mother told the girls fun, interesting stories about me when I was a little girl. Often, Alexandra and Brooke would come home and regale me with these tales, asking me lots of questions to further fill out their grandmother's vivid memory. She became the oracle of our family history, singing praises, reliving colorful, lively memories, bragging about me at every turn. She continuously reinforced to the girls how much she not only loved me, but how full of admiration she was for the way I have lived and for my design ability. She was a natural. She knew where to rub, when to hug, and how to bless with loving kindness.

> *Sure I love the dear silver that shines in your hair,/And the brow that's all furrowed, and wrinkled with care./I kiss the dear fingers, so toilworn for me.*
>
> *— Rida Johnson Young*

Mother amazed me with her thoughtfulness and insights about the girls' well-being. She had an intuitive faith that all was and would be OK, and believed I was a superb mother and knew what to do as well as what not to do. She saw my daughters as perfect angels. In her eyes they could do no wrong. She was amazingly consistent in her praise, telling me often what creative geniuses they were. I noticed that in this relationship my mother didn't expect her grandchildren to live out her dreams as she did with her own children. She was free to respond to them as they were, pure and simple. Mothers do not always have the experience to know the difference between what really matters and what is secondary to a child's well-being.

I guess grandmothers have moved on to another place, perhaps a more spiritual place, because time has taught them how to transcend the trials and tribulations of everyday life with children. A mother learns on the job, advancing through her own mistakes, but a grandmother is a seasoned professional. Grandchildren become a grandmother's second chance to mother, without all the day-to-day responsibilities for discipline. This allows her to make more room to allow her grandchildren to be themselves. As a Monarch butterfly, her colors dazzle as she flutters around her grandchildren lightheartedly, landing here and there with grace.

Practice is the best of all instructors.

— Publilius Syrus

Alexandra and Brooke revere my mother. Even though she died when Alexandra was thirteen and Brooke eleven, her importance to their lives remains vital even today. I think about her influence on them often. Her sense of humanity, her decency, her drama, and her energy for beauty are alive within the girls' being. Their fondest memories of my mother are varied and numerous, but all of them are vivid, specific, and spirited. Mother gave her all to her time with her "grands," and the energy was infectious.

Mother drew the girls into her life, abandoning her clients in order to be with them. When it rained or when the spirit moved them, they'd leave "The Studio" and go to the office, where they would sit on the floor and "scheme." Treating the girls as interns, Mother would train them to put room materials together, integrating rug samples, paint colors, fabrics, woods, and hardware selections. She did that with me when I was little, too, and I have that to thank for the faith I have in my own judgment about the visual world.

Whenever Mother asked for my opinion, I'd tell her what I thought, and when my ideas became implemented, when I saw results from my brainstorms, it was quite exciting, especially because I was so young. Once, when Alexandra picked out a robin's-egg blue for the bedroom of one of Mother's clients, she accompanied her grandmother to show the sample to the client, who approved it. Weeks later, Alexandra was taken over to the house to see the entire room painted in this cheerful, warm shade of blue. "Your color is dreamy, darling Alexandra," Mother proudly said in front of the client. Alexandra smiled, and said, "I know. It is. This is such a happy shade of blue." While Alexandra doesn't decorate professionally, she's gifted at creating her own rooms with moods inspired from nature. Both Alexandra and Brooke are amazingly visual — no simple coincidence.

The mind of a sage is the mirror of heaven and earth in which all things are reflected.

— Chuang-tzu

Mother turned everything, all times, into major events. One of her favorite expressions was, "I never do things in half measures." She gardened with the girls, allowing them to help create stone sculptures. Their paintings were framed. Baking was

If a grandmother wants to put her foot down, the only safe place to do it these days is in a notebook.

— Florida Scott-Maxwell

a process where simple ingredients were blended into awesome results, far too beautiful to merely eat. Cookies were Matisse-like cutout designs with vibrant candy-sugar coatings. Mother set the stage, played classical music, and everyone donned chintz aprons for the "bake-ins." Someone once told me that people never remember anything mediocre. Mother never understood the meaning of the word mediocre. The girls' energy for life, for giving, for loving, was fired by their grandmother's love and excitement with them; and it affects all the relationships they have with others today.

The girls have great memories of their time together. They used to beg me to take them to Westport to visit their grandmother. And in turn, they were certainly *grand* to her.

Seeing my mother's transformation from being a parent with a kind of grim fortitude to a grandmother who was serene and luminous has made me truly believe that grandmothers are enlightened parents. I often wonder if my mother would have handled me with the same sense of loving, pressure-free ease as she did my girls if she had had an opportunity to raise *me* a second time. I believe she would have.

Maternal Love Across Generations

It was a sweet experience for me to discover that Mother's newfound gentleness and tenderness was not only a revelation, but also a very real support to me as a young mother. Mother helped me to feel more relaxed. Having raised her own children, she had the unshakable understanding that you can never love too much, or praise a child enough for his or her achievements. She understood the roots of self-esteem and self-confidence. Mother wasn't critical of my parenting style, nor was she insistent that I follow her ways, which were quite different. She had been quite strict with me. Like most mothers of her generation, she *told* her children what to do rather than ask. I, on the other hand, try to take cues from my children and give them the opportunity to make decisions along with me, which allows them more freedom of expression and spontaneity. Mother never got in my way as a mother and she was always generous with her time and her talents.

Wisdom never lies.

— Homer

The anthropologist Ashley Montagu discussed in *Going Bonkers* magazine the kind of happiness that can be forged across generations:

> It is merely a matter of having to rediscover yourself, at whatever age you may be, to remake yourself, and to work to bring about a new kind of relationship between generations—for there is nothing like the wisdom of age and the inexperience of youth to engender a creative fellowship.

A smile that glowed

— John Milton

My mother and I did succeed in forming a kind of "creative fellowship" when she evolved from mother to grandmother. The wisdom and freedom she gained with age helped me enjoy turning to her for occasional advice. She always assured me that the girls were capable of expressing their own needs and interests, reminding me that all children are different, each a unique soul. I think she felt I had turned out all right and that the girls were really in secure, well-seasoned hands. I suppose she felt that now she could simply relax and enjoy their company, and let her love flow freely.

Overcoming me with the light of a smile...

— Dante

The year before my mother died, my friend Helen gave me some wise and wonderful advice. She told me to talk to Mother and ask her a billion questions. Grandmothers, after all, are the keepers of history. Mother knew the family story. She threaded each story together like a string of graduated pearls. If we hadn't talked before she died, I would have lost that great story forever. Mother was physically weak in her last year and in chronic pain from cancer. But she was able to relive moments of her youth, and told me great tales about her heyday. When she talked about these times, the pain left her face and she smiled. One day she told me:

I loved becoming an accomplished horseback rider. When I won several blue ribbons and silver trophies in Madison Square Garden at a horse show, I felt exhilaration I never thought possible. The jumps were my challenges. In my own way, I'm a daredevil. I loved the difficulty, the adventure, the potential danger, and the grace all thrown into a sport. Degas is one of my favorite artists, perhaps because we share a mutual love of horses.

Mother told me about falling in love with my father, and how handsome he was; how they'd go on sunset boat rides up and down the Charles River in Cambridge, Massachusetts, holding hands and tenderly kissing in the pink dusk. Instead of bitterness, her memories were suffused with a sense of gratitude, because together she and my father had created us, her children. And there I was, her daughter, sitting by her side.

I chose not to take the girls with me to the hospital during those final months. I wanted them to remember their grandmother as they knew her before she became terminally ill. I told her all about what the girls were up to. I took tremendous comfort in watching Mother's eyes as she listened to every detail about the girls' school, dance class, art projects, sleep-over dates, and their friends. Our time together was so peaceful and loving. I wanted her to know that she had had a second "heyday" when she became a *"grand."*

The earth is my mother—and on her bosom I will recline.

— Tecumseh

Our mothers who are now grandmothers have a lot to give us. They understand the Sisyphean ordeals of motherhood. When the girls were little, I remember phoning Mother from work one day in tears. I had been dealing with a demanding client all morning and had been up all night with Brooke, who had had an upset stomach. That afternoon, Mother arrived in New York from Connecticut supposedly "to see a client." We met for tea at the Woman's Exchange, a hangout for interior designers. She held my hands across the table and gradually I began to feel all the tension slip away. Her being there assured me that everything was going to work out. I hadn't asked her to come to my rescue, but somehow, she intuitively knew that her empathy and comfort were needed.

Enlightenment is like the moon reflected on the water.

— Dogen

When we have children of our own, we enter into a special

> *There is a divine core in human personality which each of us can realize directly, and...making this discovery is the real goal of our lives.*
>
> *— Eknath Easwaran*

bond with our own mothers. Since they already know the joys and trials of motherhood, our mothers can become our confidantes. Our mothers also may intuit when we need a break and may turn up just in time to alleviate the pressure. Certainly not all grandmothers are equally supportive. Some of us have to deal with the painful reality of disapproving mothers. But for the most part, in my travels I've met many grandmothers who know how to lift their daughters up just when they get stuck or become discouraged.

But most important of all, our mothers encourage us not to drive ourselves too hard. They remind us to take care of ourselves, too. After all, we were once their little girls.

The Sweet Blossoming of Our Own Fruit

Like many mothers with grown children, I cannot wait to become a grandmother myself. I feel I have reached the grandmother stage of my life, grateful to have Peter's grandchildren to love and adore, and eager for the arrival of Alexandra and Brooke's children, when they marry and start their own families.

I'm beginning to long for the awesome experience of witnessing the fruition of the seeds I planted. We mothers are like gardeners. We get dirty, we get our feet wet and muddy, we cut our fingers, we strain our backs, tending to what we know is valuable, what we believe is important, what we understand is our responsibility. And then we have to let go. Then, as if by the magic of the gods, a purple crocus appears in our front yard, peaking out from under the snow. Our hearts leap. Having a grandchild is the sweet blossoming and the ripened fruit of all your hard work.

My friend John told me not long ago, "We're building a swimming pool. Just another lure for the grandchildren." I laughed, because not one of John's three children is even married.

When I turned fifty, the reality of reaching the profound half-century mark made me reflect on the first five decades of my life. What does it mean to be a human being? Where am I on my journey? What are my greatest joys? What have been my deepest sorrows? What are my regrets? By meditating on the rhythms of my life, I realized how Zen-calm I've become now that my spirited, wonderful daughters are grown-ups and lead independent lives. The anticipation of becoming a grandmother fills me with radiance and effervescence.

Is achieving this "grandmother state of mind" a rite of passage for women? I think back to the way I raised Alexandra and Brooke and believe there was a definite touch of the grandmother spirit in me already. It was easy for me to allow them to be themselves. I followed their lead. But still, as I watch women with

They love because they are loving persons, in the same way that they are kind, honest...because it is in their nature to be so....

— *Abraham Maslow*

There is a wisdom of the head, and... a wisdom of the heart.

— *Charles Dickens*

their grandchildren, many seem to have an air of peace and serenity exclusive to the province of grandmotherhood—and indeed it does seem a more spiritual place.

Anticipating Life as a Grandmother

When Peter and I were at a local antiques fair in Stonington Village recently, we both fell in love with an old high chair and a tiny white christening dress stitched with delicate embroidery. We bought them both and took them home. We keep the beautiful old high chair in our kitchen. Far too beautiful to be kept in a box, the dress hangs on a fabric-covered hanger from a brass hook on my closet door. The starched white baby dress looks beautiful against the old toast-colored pine doors we stripped when we bought our eighteenth-century cottage. I keep the closet door open, just so I can appreciate this dress, which is truly a work of art in white cotton. I actually have two christening dresses. A lady in England sent me one that's an antique from her husband's side of the family. It was given in appreciation for my books, which she enjoys reading. I often enjoy looking at these two inspiring white dresses, with their long skirts full of delicate handwork, love, and family history. Old houses have few closets. Mine is in the upstairs sitting room, which is private and off limits to everyone but family. This is a sweet, quiet place where I like spending calm solitary moments, or watching movies with my family by the warm glow of the fire.

When I look at these dresses, I feel charmed by the wonder

> *The Infinite Goodness has such wide arms that it takes whatever turns to it.*
>
> *— Dante*

of the grandchildren who will one day wear them at their christenings. When my friend Eleanor had a baby recently, I quickly inquired if she wanted to borrow one of these dresses for Florence's christening. When Brooke and Alexandra saw me with the gowns, they simultaneously burst into laughter and shouted, "Pressure!" I don't mind their embarrassment. Of course I'm excited about the possibility of my daughters having children in the future. But I'm also aware that one or both may ultimately choose not to become mothers, a choice that I would respect. In any case, nothing can stop me from bubbling over with affection for each new generation!

Great wisdom is generous.

— Chuang-tzu

A Grandmother's Pride

For now, I can enjoy being a grandmother to Peter's daughters' children. Spending time with Julia, age nine, and Hillary and James, who are both six, brings us such joy. We are truly blessed. Last year, Peter and I were invited to Grandparents' Day at The Spence School in New York, with an invitation designed by our dear little Julia, who was then in the third grade. When we arrived at her homeroom, we were all asked to write a paper about what it means to be a grandparent. Julia urged us to raise our hands and read our essay to the gathering. Peter began by reading about continuity. Four of our daughters had gone to Spence before Julia: Alexandra and Brooke, and Peter's daughters Andrée and Blair; three of them graduated from there.

Julia was proud, even if she was a little embarrassed, as her

> Wisdom is the reward you get for a lifetime of listening when you'd have preferred to talk.
>
> — Doug Larsen

grandfather stood up from a small child's chair and announced, "I'm Peter Rabbit." For my part, when it was my turn to speak, I was filled with emotion. I spoke of how scrumptious it is to be a grandparent, to experience the wonder of a child through the prism of perspective. Grandmothers leave off all the worrying.

Julia's other grandparents had flown in from Florida and California, announcing that they wouldn't miss this event "for anything in the world." The morning was packed with unexpected and delightful stimulation: *I* could learn a great deal as a third-grade student at this fine school. We did some math and I made a mistake. Julia assured me, "Everyone makes mistakes. That's how you learn." I really enjoyed the guidance counselor who taught the girls and grandparents about problem solving. She used what's called the bubble method, where you envision the problem in the center, like the hub of a wheel, and the spokes around it represent different ways of reacting to the problem. It illustrates that there is a particular consequence for each potential solution.

> Eyes on the prize
>
> — Steven E. Burt

After going to see Julia's art and ceramics across the hall, Peter left temporarily for work and Julia and I dashed back to homeroom to do some creative writing. We were given a piece of paper on which we were to write jointly about being a staple: "Describe a typical day." We wrote about a nervous pink staple that was one step from torture. We had loads of fun composing the essay and later reading it to the class. Next was a ballet recital. Watching twenty-two nine-year-olds move their bodies joyfully and rhythmically to classical music, under the direction of a professional ballerina, was deeply moving. When the girls switched to practice for the Maypole dance, which they were to perform in Central Park, the dance movements turned to brisk, continuous skipping. My mind flashed back to memories of familiar scenes with Alexandra and Brooke. I still have their ballet slippers from *their* Spence days, reminding me of their grace and dignity at such a young age. And I remembered my sister's and my own ballet classes in Westport at the local YMCA, where my mother would sit in the front row, watching her two daughters dance.

There is only one person in the world you can hope to control, and that is yourself. Work on how you respond.

— Granny of Eknath Easwaran

Tears welled up as I thought about how much my mother loved coming to Grandparents' Day. *She* was the one writing flowery essays, holding the girls on her lap, sitting in those tiny low chairs, and taking lots of pictures. My daughters were the brightest, sweetest, most attractive girls alive, and here I am feeling this same tenderness toward Julia, delighting in her every move, watching her without ever looking away.

Mother was so taken by this yearly event that when she asked me to plan her funeral, she wanted Scott Joplin's "The Entertainer" played at the recessional because that was the piano music she'd heard at assembly every Grandparents' Day with the girls. There, at that dance class, my mother came alive for me, flooding my memory with the past and all the generations of children.

After taking lots of pictures and saying our good-byes to so many familiar faces—teachers, grandparents, and Julia's

So absolute she seems/ And in herself complete, so well to know/ Her own, that what she wills to do or say,/ Seems wisest, virtuousest, discreetest, best.

— *John Milton*

mother, Blair, we dashed out into a brilliant spring day. I took a picture of Julia and Peter posing in front of a magnificent mass of red and yellow tulips that swayed in the light breeze, dazzling in the light. We went to a favorite French bistro on East Eighty-second Street, where once you walk through the door you feel transported to the South of France, a favorite part of the world for us. We sat by the window and enjoyed having Julia all to ourselves. She told me the reason she and her mother are so close is "because we're very much alike. We can tell each other everything. We trust each other."

Julia's presence took over the quiet atmosphere of the restaurant. One of the owners, Gabriel Saint-Denis, came over to say hello, grinning from ear to ear. We introduced Julia to Gabriel and told him about our morning. "How old are you, Julia?" "I'm nine. I'm in third grade." Smiling, Gabriel told her, "I have a nine-year-old son. He's a nice boy. We should get you two together someday."

Julia and I sampled an assortment of sorbets, exchanging spoon dollops to see if we could identify each flavor. We voted the banana as best, but we couldn't figure out why it looked lavender in tone. We played the flavor game with Peter, and then Gabriel told us we were right on all four flavors. After savoring delicious food and even better conversation and companionship, we walked Julia to her Friday afternoon art class, where her teacher warmly welcomed us, showing us Julia's canvas of a Hudson Valley scene.

How could we be so fortunate to have this *grand* child in our lives and our hearts? Walking home, with the sun at our backs, admiring block after block of Dutch tulips along Park Avenue, Peter put his hand through my hair and said, "Is this all there is?" We always say that when we don't think life can get any better.

Adopted Grandmother to Many

Baudelaire, the nineteenth-century French poet, reminds us that "Genius is childhood recaptured." I've long thought that my grandchildren—when they come—will help me to grow in youthful ways. Already, I feel a bit spritelike. For Christmas a few years ago Julia and Hillary gave me a box-ful of wild-colored tights—hot fuchsia, emerald green, tomato red, and indigo blue. I thought they were absolutely fabulous. While most women my age wouldn't be caught dead wear-ing such tights to exercise class, let alone among grown-ups in a social situation, I jump at the chance to show them off. I feel a childlike delight whenever I wear them. In fact, I look forward to every opportunity to look like a painter's palette!

> *As large as life and twice as natural.*
>
> — *Lewis Carroll*

I once saw a cartoon in a magazine where a doctor says to an adult clutching a huge teddy bear, "It's not enough for doc-tors to prolong life. They need to prolong childhood!" I am a firm believer in turning adults into children at every available opportunity. I look for any excuse to turn the clock back and enjoy being a child all over again. Coloring and playing make-believe are among my greatest pleasures. My cover for all of

*...being the
instrument of a
higher power
is of course
inspiration.*

— *William James*

*...jewel in the
heart*

— *Buddha*

this, since, after all I am an adult, is to become
"an adopted grandmother" to many children;
that way, I always have someone to play with.
Sometimes, I feel that children are the only
people who can keep up with me!

I have a whole entourage of them in
Stonington; I love to spoil them silly. We call
the cottage "the magic house," where anyone
can do anything and everything at any time.
Reese's candy bars are eaten *before* the peanut
butter sandwich, and no one has to finish everything on their
plate. Darcy knows she can always bring a friend over to paint
watercolors, as they happily lick on a chocolate-covered ice
cream stick. Sewell is six and plays secretary; she likes to sit at
my desk in my Zen room and speak into the phone, "Alexandra
Stoddard, Incorporated. May I help you?" If she wants to pretend she's sick, she can mess up Alexandra's
bed in the room off the living room. She pre-
tends to be the ailing princess, and I bring her
Orangina and flowers, until she wants to race
around the backyard, that is, to play ball with
balloons or have a tea party—"high tea" style,
twelve swizzle sticks per cup. Whether a child
plays on my antique rocking horse, jumps up
and down on our bed, crawls under our bed,
hides, dresses up, or plays store with our old English cash reg-
ister, children are always welcome in our cottage —or wherever
we are. Even in the elevator of our apartment building in New
York, I often feel like the pied piper.

I feel so lucky to have so many young friends, to be able to
spend time with them at play and in my imagination. I adore

being a grandmother figure in their lives. I never fear that I'm spoiling them too much; I believe that whenever a child is genuinely loved, he or she will share that same affection and warmth with others.

The Support Staff

I'd like to give credit and thanks here to all the women in my life who have, in one way or another, been mother figures for me, women who have cared about me, loved me, and gently guided me through all the hailstorms and dangerous seas of motherhood.

No one woman can be all things to a child. My mother's gifts to me were plentiful, but there were some things she simply couldn't provide. I don't fault her for that.

During my adolescence, Connie, my future (first) mother-in-law (I had known Connie since I was a teenager and met her son—later my tennis partner and then husband—on the tennis court), introduced me not only to the world of good food, but she helped shape my interest in good literature. These passions continue to enrich my life, all these years afterward. We met when I was thirteen, and she and I enjoyed reading the same authors, many of whom she introduced to me. I was young and impressionable, and my mind was open. I devoured Ernest Hemingway, F. Scott Fitzgerald, Mark Twain, Henry Miller, D. H. Lawrence, Dostoyevsky, Anton Chekhov,

Love like this will plunge us into deepest consciousness and release in us the power to make a lasting contribution to all of life.

— Eknath Easwaran

Stendhal, Lawrence Durrell, Gerald Durrell, Henry James, Edith Wharton, Colette, Eudora Welty, Virginia Woolf, Willa Cather, and Anaïs Nin. At the time, I had no clue that I would become a writer. So much of what I read was fiction, which I now rarely read and have never written myself. But those books fed me, fascinated me, and as I now realize, were the roots of my career as a writer. Connie was attracted to my thirst for knowledge and my passion for reading anything I could get my hands on. In my free time, I would go to the study off the terrace of their Victorian house and pick out a book from Connie's library, inevitably one that she had read. She was very protective of her library, once reprimanding a friend of mine for borrowing one of the four volumes of Lawrence Durrell's *Alexandria Quartet* without her knowledge. Connie and I would have lively and lengthy discussions about all the books we read. While my mother inspired my aesthetic sense, Connie saw a literary spark in me and ignited it. Her genuine interest in my intellectual cultivation when I was an adolescent was a major catalyst in my development as an artist.

Renounce and enjoy!

— Mahatma Gandhi

My aunt Betty Johns, though she never had children of her own, was one of the most maternal women I ever had the honor to know intimately. Her role in my spiritual quest is unequaled. Aunt Betty opened my eyes to the vast spiritual beliefs of the world, and the firm conviction that women could accomplish anything they set their minds to. She taught me that though our cultural roots may differ, we still want essentially the same things of life: goodness, kindness, and love. Had Aunt Betty not given me her spiritual guidance, I would have remained a plow horse in a field with blinders on, without depth perception or peripheral vision. I would have remained completely provincial, knowing only the closed society in which I was raised, and the only religious experience I would have had was the doctrine of the Episcopal church. Betty's father was a Methodist minister, a path she would have likely followed had she been born male. Instead, she decided to focus on world spirituality, becoming an international social worker. She took sincere and devoted interest in nurturing the souls of her nieces through books such as Erich Fromm's *The Art of Loving,* William James's *The Varieties of Religious Experience,* and later Dag Hammarskjold's *Markings* and Rollo May's *Love and Will,* and took us all on a life-changing trip around the world, revealing to us the poorest yet most spiritually beautiful places on earth.

I speak the truth, not my fill of it, but as much as I dare speak; and I dare to do so a little more as I grow old.

— Michel de Montaigne

I lived with Betty for several months while I was in Manhattan, studying design at the New York School of Design. Unmarried and self-employed, she was extremely independent, and free to travel a great portion of the year. She had a broader, more liberal view of life in general than the rest of the family because of her worldly experience. She had friends from all over the world. She introduced me to people from Pakistan, Burma (now Myanmar), Ceylon (now Sri Lanka), and other countries, mostly Asian, where she spent her sabbaticals. She used to take me to parties at the United Nations, where I'd be the only "local."

Wisdom sails with wind and tide.

— John Florio

Because Betty never married or had children, she was able to focus a lot of attention on her nieces and nephews. She sent us all long letters from exotic places. She wrote from Tahiti about her World Council of Churches Conference in Geneva, where she was the only woman. When the keynote speaker rose, the first words out of his mouth were, "Good morning, gentlemen." In true Aunt Betty fashion, she began her speech in front of the same audience with, "Good Morning, ladies." She would tell stories beginning with statements such as, "Two days ago I was on an elephant." I remember her letter from Agra, India, in which she wrote that she had just seen the Taj Majal and dreamed that she would soon take me there (and she did!). She described in detail the mosaics of semiprecious stones on white marble against the blue sky, remarking on the irony of such opulence amidst the most dire poverty in the world. In total, Aunt Betty corresponded with more than five hundred people, mostly women and children.

> *The one great thing about growing old is that nothing is going to lead to anything. Everything is of the moment.*
>
> *— Joseph Campbell*

When Aunt Betty was not traveling I spent a lot of time with her because we lived in the same city. Her influence on me continues to grow as I reflect on her wisdom and her example as a fulfilled woman. Her active concern for the common good and her avid social consciousness made Betty an example of someone who lived out her own higher vision of life. I have so many memories and photographs of our time together, wearing saris, riding in fourth class trains in India, worshipping at Buddhist temples. Aunt Betty was truly wild and unconventional, but also one of the most real women I have ever known. I'm reminded of her wonderfully free spirit each time I read Dr. Seuss's *Oh, the Places You'll Go!* to our grandchildren:

Today is your day!
Your mountain is waiting
So...get on your way!

My spiritual sage, John Coburn, went to seminary with my aunt. Now John and I are bound to each other by our mutual love for Betty.

I was delighted to learn that one of my readers also found a mother in her maiden aunt. Sharon writes:

I grew up next door to my grandmother and grandfather and their daughter, Aunt Lois. When I was a little girl, Aunt Lois would take me to see the *Nutcracker*...the world of ballet opened before my eyes. She would take me to plays — the world of theater opened my mind.... She would take me on vacations to the sandy California beaches, giving me endless hours to skip the waves, letting grainy sand hourglass through my fingers, and listening to the poetry inside a seashell; she took me to Sun Valley, where we ate campfire-roasted trout, and danced through meadows gathering sunflowers.... These free-spirited adventures opened my eyes to a larger world, different cultures, a vision beyond my immediate cloistered surroundings. Aunt Lois feathered my nest with a love of the arts and travel adventure at a very tender age.

The journey not the arrival matters.

— Michel de Montaigne

My godmother Mitzi Christian was also a significant, adopted maternal figure in my life, and one who was there for me at times when my own mother could not be. When Mother refused to listen to my argument for my attending art school

Some persons are born with an inner constitution which is harmonious and well-balanced from the onset. Their impulses are consistent with one another, their will follows without trouble the guidance of their intellect, their passions are not excessive, and their lives are little haunted by regrets.

— William James

over Smith College upon my graduation from prep school, Mitzi patiently heard me out and helped convince Mother that it was the right choice for me. I learned so much from her about how a happy adult can pass that happiness on to a child. She treated me with enormous respect by always making me feel that what I had to say was important. She was a very "hands-off" person who never tried to tell me what to do, and who never disabused me of the notion that I could do certain things better than others.

Mitzi was a happy, fulfilled woman. She loved life, was healthy, happily married, had loving children, and a successful career as an artist. She was extremely beautiful, strong, and feminine in a handsome way. She had great personal style. She integrated everything into a life that seemed bigger, more noble, more civilized than most.

Mitzi and her husband, Frank, loved and adored each other for life. The atmosphere at their eighteenth-century homestead, "Meetinghouse Farm," was intoxicatingly vibrant with their love and energy. I remember Frank and Mitzi, both wearing jodhpurs, looking so fit and trim in high leather boots that gleamed through the fresh saddle dust after a long ride. Their house had a grand front hall, lit by windows on either side of the entrance door. The other end of the house opened up to a lawn and enormous trees, seen through wide windows and a door leading to the terrace. Whenever Mitzi came into the hall carrying her cutting shears and a basket of freshly cut flowers from her garden, Frank would walk through the front door and meet her halfway for a kiss. They had an ear for each other's presence and took every opportunity to show affection and love.

Mitzi became a real model to me of what a happy life might consist of for a woman. She was well educated, an accomplished artist, a trustee of the Fine Arts Museum of Boston, well educated, and a great traveler. Her greatest love was for Oriental art and culture, but it was her tenderness, her femininity, and her gentleness that had the greatest impact on me. Her radiant smile made me feel that I was important to her.

This kind of joy comes with a life that is carried on to the best of one's ability, with the faith or confidence that this is what one is meant to do.

— John Bowen Coburn

I also feel fortunate to have found a grandmother figure in Eleanor McMillen Brown, my mentor and first employer. I never had the opportunity to establish close relationships with my own two grandmothers; both had died by the time I turned seven, and had lived too far away for frequent visits. My personal relationship with Mrs. Brown developed alongside our professional one, and there is no doubt that she was one of the seminal women in my life.

What I admired most in Eleanor Brown was her gentleness and her regal bearing. She was very self-disciplined. She kept strict work hours, and was never late—always early—to an appointment. But discipline never prevented her from tasting all of life's pleasures. When she was well into her eighties she still enjoyed having one chilled martini before dinner. And she always ended her meal with a little sweet, usually a small dish of coffee ice cream. She told me little secrets that have stood up well to the test of time. Mrs. Brown was also a generous soul. When I was seven months pregnant with Alexandra, I traveled to St. Louis with Mrs. Brown for a decorating job. I had hidden my pregnancy well behind A-line dresses, but during this trip, I finally confessed, adding in the same sentence how important my career was to me and how much I wanted to continue with it. Mrs. Brown smiled and said, soothingly, "Oh Sandie, we'll work it out." After Alexandra and Brooke were born, she used to come to all our main family events, including Easter and Thanksgiving, because her husband had died and her only son lived too far away to visit frequently. She watched me raise my children.

Mrs. Brown had very definite ideas on food too: "The more common the lettuce, the finer it should be chopped," or "Add a few teaspoons of sour cream to Hellmann's mayonnaise and it will taste homemade." When she spoke of fashion and dress, she told me, "I either spend money on really fine clothes or buy modestly priced items. There is no middle range if you want to have true style." She believed a woman with a good figure could wear an inexpensive dress as long as it was simple and handsomely tailored. "No frills," she'd say with a shudder. "A woman should wear good shoes that fit her. Most women pretend they have smaller feet than they do. Sandie, if your feet aren't comfortable, you can't move through life effortlessly." Her walks were legendary. (Her feet were obviously comfortable.) She also believed a woman's handbag should be attractive and large enough to be useful. "Sandie, we 'ladies' need something big enough to carry a measuring tape, a scale ruler,

> Who then are the true philosophers? Those who are lovers of the vision of truth.
>
> — Plato

a notepad, a handkerchief, as well as tissue to clean our shoes." Mrs. Brown always cleaned her shoes after a visit to a dusty job site, and carried a spare pair of white gloves, just in case the first pair got dirty.

Mrs. Brown was a lady, through and through. She did everything gracefully, loving every opportunity to appreciate detail and refinement, beauty, color, and art. She was a mother who had had her share of heartaches; her son struggled with cancer, her first marriage failed, and her second ended with the death of her husband from emphysema. But I never once heard her complain. She'd reminisce, remembering happy scenes from earlier days. Generations older than I, she was a key maternal figure in my life, a beautiful, lovely lady.

> *Dignity does not consist in possessing honors, but in deserving them.*
>
> *— Aristotle*

I'll never forget seeing *The Belle of Amherst* with her, when Julie Harris played Emily Dickinson. Mrs. Brown had already seen the play, but she thought we should go see it together. After the theater, we went to the Four Seasons, sat by a fountain, sipped a glass of chablis and ate littleneck clams. In fact, I see a certain connection between Mrs. Brown and Emily Dickinson. Though she was as fiercely private as Dickinson was, she intimated much about her life nonetheless, including her spirituality. She was the woman who taught me to "church hop," encouraging me to accompany her to all different types of services, to absorb all the good from a certain preacher's sermon, or simply to listen to a different point of view.

> *The great good is wisdom.*
>
> *— St. Augustine*

> *...I am amazed at my increased energy and vigor of mind; at my strength to meet situations of all kinds; and at my disposition to love and appreciate everything.... All at once the whole world has turned good to me.*
>
> — Horace Fletcher

Her contributions to my life continue to grow, even though she died five years ago. Her example showed me how to have confidence in myself. I remember how, in her late seventies, she walked up five flights of stairs to my apartment to deliver a yellow sweater and bonnet for newborn Alexandra. But of course, she had lots of practice, since daily she had climbed her way up to my office on the top floor of her townhouse headquarters, bracelets jingling, and asked, "Any probs today?" Her quiet poise, dignity, and ready compliments and eagerness to share all she learned found a secure place in my soul. I often ask myself, "What would Mrs. Brown say?" or "What would Mrs. Brown do?" Her presence is still here as a model, a guide, and as a grand lady whose influence on my life means even more to me now in my maturity. Although she didn't try to look younger than she was, she admired youth. She grew more beautiful with each year, and with the arrival of every grandchild, every great-grandchild.

A woman who lived from 1890 to 1990, five days shy of her 101st birthday, Mrs. Brown undoubtedly had a lot to teach us. She never wrote for publication and rarely spoke in public, but her life delivered long, long years of maternal instinct tuned up to a higher pitch. She never used a heavy hand, and her favorite clients were kind, gracious mothers. Family life is what had attracted her to residential design. She always nurtured my design career as a mother would, challenging me, yet taking pride in my work. Her encouragement and faith in me never wavered, and she knew as well as I did when it was time for me to "leave the nest" and start a design firm of my own. I believe I was the daughter she never had.

Mrs. Brown seemed to glide through her days with a sense of ease and feminine grace, rare and remarkable at the end of the twentieth century. She was a maternal soul at heart; she had a calm and gentle nature that never deviated from this, her great source of strength.

Phyl Gardner takes her own special place as another nurturing woman in my life. Just shy of my fifteenth birthday, this little, jolly English lady came into my life to teach me about art at the Mary A. Burnham School, a prep school for Smith College in Northampton, Massachussetts. Phyl was an art-history teacher who never had children of her own. Instead, she felt that all her students were hers to love and influence. Now I realize that her greatest abilities were exercised outside her classroom and her art studio, in her home, an old farmhouse near the school, where she lived with Jimmy, an architect.

I used to hang out at her studio on the farm, where I had my own space. She would draw and paint while I worked on my own creations; sometimes she would talk to me about my future. She told me I had talent, and that Smith was not the right place for me to nurture it. She encouraged me to "follow my dreams."

Whenever I visited them on weekends, I loved to sleep in a small room off the kitchen. Phyl would knock on my door after I'd come in for the night, bringing me a little tray with hot milk and vanilla sugar cookies. "This will give you sweet dreams," she would giggle. Some

Nature, time and patience are the three great physicians.

— Anonymous

women, often teachers, nurture many, many young people, giving them a special love outside the bonds of home. It's a love that many children seek because it connects them to the larger world, and is not contingent on family ties. From this, children gain a real sense of being loved for who they are. Phyl Gardner represented this love. What a funny, happy lady.

> *Thought is the strongest thing we have. Work done by true and profound thought—that is a real force.*
>
> *— Albert Schweitzer*

The tenderness and maternal support given by friends to our children is one of the deepest connections we as mothers can have. Actress Marsha Mason became a close friend of Peter's and mine when she hired me to decorate her penthouse apartment in New York. Marsha chose to be a devoted stepmother to her husband Neil Simon's two daughters. Even after the couple divorced, she and the girls have maintained a close, affectionate friendship. Marsha adores Alexandra and Brooke and has never lost an opportunity to connect with them, bringing them gifts, or taking them out to lunch. Some friends ask you how your children are, but others *need* to know. Marsha really cares about our daughters. This genuine affection is equal to motherly love. It is a tremendously important source of strong, positive support to a child (and to her mother).

When my daughters' father remarried, his second wife, Mary Ann, had no children. Together they embraced the opportunity to love and nurture Alexandra and Brooke. Mary Ann is a journalist and became a role model for Alexandra's career as a writer. In our extended family we really respect, love, and care deeply about one another. Once, many years ago, I overheard the girls telling friends about their family and what they said made me cry. They told their friends how fortunate they were to have four loving parents when most people only have two.

I am deeply gratified that my girls can give love to and receive maternal love from so many different women. It reminds me that we all have so much to give one another, and how much we all need one another. As mothers, we can take comfort from the fact that throughout their lives, our children will have many mothers to whom they can turn when need be. They will never be wholly dependent on us. As Alexandra and Brooke connect with other mentors and sources of maternal influence, our love will remain centered—wherever they are, wherever I am. But I also know that none of us goes through life alone; the more love we give, the more love we receive. Everyone matters.

Large, divine, and comfortable words

— Alfred, Lord Tennyson

Chapter 8

The Album of Continuity

Let me not forget that I am the daughter of a woman...who herself never ceased to flower, untiringly, during three quarters of a century.

—Colette

The Rhythms of Maternal Love

When I was cleaning out my mother's house after she died, I came across my white quilted baby book tucked neatly on a library shelf. It was resting next to baby books for each of my siblings, together with Mother's Bible. Along with locks of our hair, these meticulously documented scrapbooks had been kept by Mother, where she had mounted hundreds of photographs on black construction paper with white corner tabs, labeled with all the pertinent information, including the dates, in white ink. In a rush to pack up all the boxes and get everything ready for the movers, I didn't take time to look through the book then, but my heart pounded with excitement. I wanted to wait until I could savor the experience. Even though I was the third of four children in my fam-

The eternal female draws us onward.

— Goethe

ily, Mother still recorded every detail about the first year of my life. She tracked the progress of my weight and height, saved notes of congratulations on my birth, listed all the presents received, and then, of course, there was the abundance of baby pictures. What a treasure these books are to me and to Alexandra and Brooke.

A Document of Maternal Love

The week before my brother Powell's memorial service in Chicago, I pored through family pictures, reliving moments of our childhood in Connecticut with my older brother. I found snapshots of everything: going off to camp in Maine together in the summer, playing tennis, family Christmas parties, bike rides, softball games, class pictures, and family portraits. Rather than making me feel sad, these photographs reminded me of the close relationship Powell and I had, and all the good times we spent together. Mother's photo archives helped me to understand and appreciate our history together, and realize the impact of our actions on each other's separate lives, which I would otherwise not have fully known. I am so grateful to my mother for recording the chronology of our growing up as brother and sister, helping me to recognize Powell's indelible imprint on me.

> The strands are all there: to the memory nothing is ever really lost.
>
> — Eudora Welty

A mother's presence lives forever. She has the ability to influence the generations to come, guiding our path with the legacy she left behind. Like our mothers before us, we do so many things to express our love for our children, never fully aware when we do them of their eventual impact on future generations. Long after we're gone, our descendants will discover more and more clues about who we and our families were and what they may have inherited from us.

When I was a young mother, we could buy little pocket notebooks for fifteen cents. I remember stocking up at the five-and-dime store on these booklets, which I filled so quickly, I never seemed to have enough on hand. I jotted down all the adorable utterances that came from the lips of Alexandra and Brooke. I dated each page so that the thought and scene were captured for all time. I followed my mother's example of dating everything in addition to recording the location of where we were and with whom. This detail really comes in handy years later when you attempt to piece together all the fragments of your life and of your children's early years. Although I did not give it much thought at the time, I now understand that these miniature scrapbooks I collected as a young mother have become priceless archives for my family. They are part of my legacy, my contribution to the continuity of family life. They will give my grandchildren clues about themselves and where they came from.

Ever since I traveled around the world at the age of sixteen, I have always taken a camera along wherever my travels take me. I like to capture the mood and flavor of a place, focusing my lens on its scenery, architecture, and people. I love to capture the spon-

> *He wove a web in childhood, / A web of sunny air.*
>
> — Charlotte Brontë

> *The one who thinks over his experiences most, and weaves them into systematic relations with each other, will be the one with the best memory.*
>
> — William James

taneity in life. Having a strong visual sense is a significant part of my family heritage. Not only was my mother an interior designer who also painted and sculpted, but my uncle painted, and my older sister was a professional photographer for years. I was raised in an environment attuned to aesthetics, which encouraged me to see and appreciate all the beauty available to us in life.

Family faces are magic mirrors. Looking at people who belong to us, we see the past, present and future.

— Gail Lumet Buckley

My most beloved pictures are of me, peach fuzz on my head, when I was less than a year old. I keep one of these baby snapshots in a silver frame on my writing table. I find it moving to see myself at the start of my life. Peter's favorite childhood picture of himself was taken on Carlyle Avenue in Babylon, Long Island, in 1924, when he was four. The photo is in black and white, but Peter remembers the colors vividly. He was wearing a knee-length French-blue linen smock with white cuffs and collar adorned with detailed handwork made by Miriam, Peter's mother. It rests on Peter's closet ledge, framed in gold leaf, so he can see it every morning and every night. The resemblance between Peter and his daughters Blair and Andrée and their children at the same age is uncanny.

The Poetry of Continuity

I love looking at early pictures of me alongside early childhood pictures of Alexandra and Brooke. The sense of continuity and connection it gives me is powerful, though one can feel this continuity in so many other ways. We needn't be the biological mothers to experience the universal sense of continuity we feel when looking at *our* children.

There is one picture, though, that I adore. It is a picture of me taken when I was seven, wearing a seersucker pinafore of periwinkle blue and white. Mother loved seersucker. She had blanket coverlets in the summer in soft pastel shades of this classic material. The boys had yellow, my sister and I had mint green, the guest rooms had pink and blue. The photograph of me in the seersucker pinafore was in black and white, but, like Peter, I remember that dress and its colors vividly. Mother had made this dress and a matching one for my sister. I remember when her friend came to take professional photographs of us. I felt so pretty in my new dress.

The second summer Peter and I were married, we took a family trip to France, ending up in Provence, after exploring Paris. Brooke was five at the time and Alexandra was eight. We alternated between four-star meals where we made a long pilgrimage by car to seek out the great chefs of France, and picnics on the side of the road in tiny villages along the way. One day, we ended up picnicking in Châteauneuf-du-Pape, in a vineyard with plump purple grapes warmed by the sun, ripening before our eyes. While the girls and I filled our basket with baguettes, tomatoes, ham, cheese, niçoise olives, peach tarts, wine, and chilled Oranginas, I asked the woman in the general store of this charming twelfth-century town if the wine was local. *"Ici. Ici."* She pointed to the floor with

> *When you look at your life, the greatest happinesses are family happinesses.*
>
> — Dr. Joyce Brothers

> *I would like them to be the happy end of my story.*
>
> — Margaret Atwood

> *The tie which links mother and child is of such pure and immaculate strength as to be never violated. Holy, simple, and beautiful in its construction, it is the emblem of all we can imagine of fidelity and truth; it is the blessed tie whose value we feel in the cradle, and whose loss we lament on the verge of the grave.*
>
> *— Washington Irving*

her forefinger. The wine was made in the basement of her store. You can't get more local than that.

When Alexandra, Brooke, and I had finished our gathering, we found Peter sitting in the square sketching the local scene like a native. We walked past the stone fountain, refreshed by the breeze spraying a mist of water our way on this sultry August day. Off to the vineyard we went, several hundred skips and jumps away. I was the designated driver that day so I sipped Orangina from a yellow straw and spread out a beautiful patchwork quilt. Having decorated a house in Paris, I discovered the French have an affinity for American quilts and make trips to Pennsylvania to hunt them down. We found one we all fell in love with in a Paris shop and, rather than leave it in the hotel room, we took it along for these al-fresco lunches.

As the girls wandered into the vineyard, I took out my camera to capture this ideal, timeless moment. As I was clicking the camera, one particular image of Alexandra made me almost tremble with emotion. I didn't say anything at the time, but I felt as if I were gazing at myself through the camera lens. When I picked up the developed rolls of film after our return to New York, I immediately searched for the pictures I had taken of Alexandra that had stirred me so. The experience was both surreal and romantic.

I focused on the vision of Alexandra, who was dressed in a blue-and-white seersucker pinafore. I retrieved that snapshot my mother had taken of me twenty-seven years before. The photographs were spitting images of each other. I had both pictures blown up to five-by-seven inches and placed them side-by-side in a blue leather frame on an antique table in our living room. Everyone who sees those pictures is astounded and moved by our likeness at the same age.

On the wall of my childhood room there hung a muscum poster, a Renoir painting of a mother with her two little girls, all dressed alike. It reminded me of the pictures someone took of my mother on a beach in Nantucket, flanked by her two daughters wearing bathing suits of red, white, and blue stripes, which matched hers. One day, I was inspired to design a ribbon fabric that Brunschwig and Fils, a favorite international fabric house of New York interior designers, printed in five different colorways. I had a seamstress make matching sundresses for Alexandra, Brooke, and me with a cute circle cutout in the back. I have numerous photographs of us in these adorable ribbon sundresses.

Memory is the treasury and guardian of all things.

— Cicero

Last summer, I took a picture of a young, blond, Scandinavian mother with her two-year-old daughter, both dressed in Liberty of London playsuits in a floral print of pink, baby blue, yellow, and green. When I got my film back, I realized that I had never asked the woman for her address so I couldn't send her a copy. Instead, I had a print made for myself and tacked it to the "memory board" in my Zen room. I adore those pictures; the matching outfits never fail to fill me with a sense of connection between a mother and her children.

Mother had a second Renoir print in my room; this one was of a little blond girl holding a watering can, tending her garden.

Every time Peter and I visit Alexandra in Washington, we go to the National Gallery to see the original painting of this girl. She evokes such nostalgia and pleasure in me because, in a sense, I feel I am this child. I always stock up on postcards of this painting and tuck them into books or inside the top of a box of stationery or into a notebook for a little surprise encounter, as well as sending them on to childhood friends with a note of cheer.

Treasures of Continuity

Last October, I received a touching letter from Hillary, the daughter of my best friend Tess, who died of cancer when she was forty-four, the year Hillary was a senior in high school. I've loved Hillary since her birth. And now I had received this special communication, just hours before Hillary herself became a mother, giving birth to a beautiful boy, Murphey Durgin Harmon. Here was such a treasured piece of continuity.

In her letter to me, Hillary said she and her husband Murphey are expecting "the ultimate miracle, our first child!"

We are very excited, and I can't tell you how much you've been on my mind as I think of Mom, and your friendship with her—and I reread all the wonderful notes you've written to me over the years about Mom and her love for me. I have many of your precious letters…and they really are a treasure, because there are so few people who can tell me, from her standpoint, about our relationship. You wrote me a marvelous note before Murphey and I got married, with Mom's enclosed note to you, and I treasured the letter you wrote me just after our wedding.

Infinite comes to life in a finite personality to remind us what life is for.

— *Bhagavad Vita*

Hillary was always the light in Tess's heart. We spoke of our children every time we were alone. What a joy to anticipate Tess's grandchild, through her spirit. Birth has a way of bringing together all love that is the underpinning of our true humanity, our sense of appreciation, and the source of our greatest joy.

Tess's love envelops me through her darling daughter Hillary's spirit. I'm reminded of the wisdom of the Vedas, of the *Bhagavad Gita:* "In the midst of the sun is the light, in the midst of the light is the truth, and in the midst of the truth is the imperishable being."

Assembling a Childhood Archive

Given the amazing impact that pictures, including postcards, can have on our memories, what gift could be treasured more by our children than a collection of photographs and sentimental postcards stored for long-term preservation and enjoyment? Every woman is unique in the way she keeps these invaluable family records. Julia and Hillary's mother, Blair, keeps ongoing books, logging important dates and events, letters, cards, postcards, notes, and an assortment of other memorabilia. Taking pictures is a universal way of recording family history. Home movies are fun, but as with slides from a family vacation, we often feel too busy to watch them and find flipping through a stack of old photographs more enjoyable. We can tuck our favorites into our wallets, frame them, blow them up, make copies, and most important, capture a single moment.

These stories are like bonsai plants—small and particular, but in them you can see the whole world.

— Barbara Hytch

a tour guide at Hill Top, Beatrix Potter's home

Several years ago, Brooke started designing fabric-covered bulletin boards with crisscrossed ribbons so you can tuck in a picture or tack in a postcard. Not only are her creations beautiful, but they're enormously practical. We can't frame every picture, but we can tuck pictures on this board and feel moved whenever we look at them.

I have so many thousands of photographs, it's impossible to keep them *all* in scrapbooks or posted on colorful "memory" bulletin boards. I store many of them in pretty, yet sturdy, boxes of assorted sizes tied with ribbons. We have dozens of these boxes stacked on a window seat in our library, inviting hours of pleasurable time travel, reliving a trip, a birthday, or a holiday. Whenever I need a jolt of happiness, I pull out one of the boxes and revel in the smiling faces of our family. Smiling in front of the camera is an especially precious tradition—"Cheese." People are recorded in their best, happiest light.

One of my favorite, most practical discoveries is the shoe box. I have large feet and even as a young girl, pictures, letters, and postcards fit in my shoe boxes very nicely. I later realized that the five-by-seven-inch index cards I found in France and write on day and night are also the perfect size to store in my shoe boxes. I can be as organized or scattered as I want to when filing my pictures. The real bonus of these rectangular boxes is that they're a handy size to lug around. I've been known to travel with one or two so I can always look over my notes and savor favorite photographs and letters that I take along for romantic reasons. Many of our children share our sentimentality. Brooke saved every letter I wrote her the year she spent living in Paris after college and brought them home in French shoe boxes. Luckily, nowadays we can find empty, colorful containers the size of shoe boxes at several warehouse and discount stores. Otherwise, it could get quite expensive buying all those shoes!

He is blessed over all mortals who loses no moment of the passing life in remembering the past.

— Henry David Thoreau

Preserving Childhood

Someday, you and your child will get together and go through boxes of family memorabilia. I find tremendous inspiration and joy in doing so. I can lose myself for hours of time looking through photographs with my daughters. During these joyful, sentimental periods, I understand the real significance of keeping such archives. Though they provide me with so much delight, I have really preserved them for my children, so someday they can relive the times we've shared together with their own children: the card from the favorite garden shop, the menus from a restaurant, the matchbox, the postcard, and all the photographs.

Mrs. Brown once wisely gave me some sound advice about decorating that could be applied to mothering. "Be careful of what you throw away. You never know when you'll need it." I love the fact that my mother saved every letter I wrote her in my whole life. The ones from Camp Fleur de Lis in Sabego, Maine, are priceless. We couldn't eat dinner Sunday nights unless we wrote to our parents. We would have to hand our postcards or envelopes to our counselors at our cabins before going to the cookout. Secretly, we liked the routine, a habit I'm grateful to have maintained throughout my life. When I traveled around the world, I always wrote home instead of keeping a detailed journal. Those letters are irreplaceable pieces to the puzzle of my memory of great pleasures I enjoyed during those three months.

> *A picture memories bring to me: I look across the years and see myself beside my mother's knee.*
>
> *— John Greenleaf Whittier*

Mother saved everything. This is one of the ways we hold on to memories and pass them on to future generations. My mother saved her wedding veil and preserved her grandfather's christening dress with gold monogrammed buttons. She saved the champagne taffeta debutante dress I wore at the Boston cotillion. I have saved the red velvet dresses with antique lace collars that Brooke and Alexandra wore to their first family Christmas party when Brooke was two and Alexandra four.

Often, mothers collect experiences, and in doing so, preserve their children's childhoods. We hold on to finger paintings, scribbles, crib sheets, and clay creations. We save seashells and sand from family vacations, pressed flowers from celebrations and nature walks, sheet music from piano lessons, report cards, and pictures drawn on white paper doilies retrieved from under coffee cups in restaurants. We document sports events, graduations, school plays, senior proms, and birthday parties. Over time, our collections become priceless treasures, that we cherish forever.

Children Carrying on Your Traditions

Last year, Alexandra called me at the end of March. "Where will you and Peter be the second Sunday of May, Mom?" "I have no idea," I answered. "Why?" "It's Mother's Day, and Brooke and I want to take you and Peter out to lunch in New York." The year before, we were together in Washington for Mother's Day. Looking back, the girls have always made a big fuss over me on Mother's Day. "How sweet. We accept." "Great. Where do you want to go for lunch, Mom?"

Hold fast the time! Guard it, watch over it, every hour, every minute! Unregarded it slips away.... Hold every moment sacred. Give each clarity and meaning, each the weight of thine awareness, each its true and due fulfillment.

— Thomas Mann

We voted for Harry Cipriani's, a trendy, fun Italian restaurant we've been going to off and on for special family reunions. This international gathering place is on Fifth Avenue, catercorner from the Plaza Hotel and the famous Pulitzer Fountain, with Central Park just across the street, where horse-drawn carriages await their passengers at its entrance. This is simply our favorite people-watching place. A table by the window assures a view of lots of mothers with their children promenading on Fifth Avenue. When Alexandra phoned, it was sleeting, dark, and dreary, and I was joyfully anticipating this celebration in May.

> For thy sweet love remember'd such wealth brings.
>
> — William Shakespeare

"We'll wear our pastel suits and Peter can take some pictures of us. Do you have the right shade lavender stockings, Mom?" I couldn't believe my ears, remembering one of our "grooves," as we call precious, pleasant times spent together, when we each bought a different-colored pastel suit, like Jordan almonds, lilac, pink, and peach. (No one can persuade me there is no difference between men and women. Who but a female would know what she was wearing several months ahead of time?) We planned with great care what we were going to wear. When I got off the telephone with Alexandra, I went to my closet to check my purple stocking supply. I even selected a vibrant hot-pink, chartreuse, and lime-green silk scarf, bought in Florence in the sixties, designed by Emilio Pucci. As with planning a trip, the anticipation intensifies the pleasure.

> The events in our lives happen in a sequence in time but in their significance to ourselves they find their own order...the continuous thread of revelation.
>
> — Eudora Welty

Opening a drawer, looking through my collection of brightly colored, patterned scarves, made me think of my mother. Many were ones I had given her as presents, which I inherited after she died. I began to have vivid memories of my mother. I could visualize her wearing these different scarves, in her house, in our apartment, when we were together in restaurants, and at the theater.

Harry Cipriani's is located in the Sherry

Netherland Hotel. For years, Mother and I went there for lunch when it was the hotel's restaurant before it became Cipriani. We'd even gone there for Mother's Day one year. Fresh memories flooded. Our mothers always remain in our subconscious. This is a deeply poignant, soulful experience. We are imprinted by our early lives for the rest of our lives. My mother was the most constant, loving, most present person in my life. Thomas Moore, author of *Care of the Soul* and *Soul Mates: Honoring the Mysteries of Love and Relationship*, believes:

> *The most poignant recollection is Mother.*
>
> *— Peter Megargee Brown*

The relationship goes on. People still have a real presence in our lives when they're no longer physically there…as memories, mementos and family albums show as well…embracing and honoring the relationship…The people we love who are no longer alive connect us to the eternal. They bring eternity into our lives in a way that's intimate because it's part of the family; it's not abstract, yet it is quite spiritual, and that nourishes the soul.

I went about my day with a heightened awareness of how much I love my mother and Alexandra and Brooke. As the weeks passed, my expectations grew for this memorable day. Being a mother is its own reward, but warm feelings well up in me whenever my daughters make special arrangements for being together on this second Sunday of May. But even my rather vivid imagination didn't prepare me for this reunion. Our luncheon party turned out to be an epiphany of tenderness, continuity, and love. I truly felt regal, like the "Queen

Mum," as they showered me with pastel-wrapped gifts. Brooke loves working with fabric, so all the presents were shrouded in lush silks, with flowing French ribbons.

The girls had thought through everything, and of course the colors of the packages complemented our suits. They also made a bouquet of lilac, purple, and white peonies, accented by pale whitish pink and hot-pink shades, with fragrant lily of the valley tucked in. My love of lilac as well as lily of the valley verges on obsession, and when Peter and I married in May, Alexandra, Brooke, and I carried lily of the valley and wore yellow dresses. Before she died, Mother insisted, "Only peonies at my funeral, dear. Only peonies." How she knew she'd die in May in Connecticut at the height of the peony season is a mystery.

The food at Harry Cipriani's was sensational. With our aperitifs we nibbled on paper-thin, wickedly fattening zucchini chips, bit into freshly baked bread sticks and pastry swirl rolls. This was a day to celebrate, not to hold back. The mâche salad with drippings of green olive oil, balsamic vinegar, and cracked pepper, was topped by thin shavings of aged Parmesan cheese. Hot, crisp French bread toast slices appeared. The feast was off to a good start.

But when Alexandra and Brooke insisted I open my presents while waiting for our entrées, I lost it. Every gift was a picture of the girls and me, or of my mother with my sister and me. I felt I was the daughter taking Mother to a Mother's Day

When no one knows where it will end, you can possess the state. And when you possess the mother of the state, you can last a very long time. This is called having deep roots and a firm base. It's the Way of long life and long-lasting vision.

— Lao-tzu

celebration. I felt her presence. Our luncheon ceremony lasted three and a half hours, ending with lots of espresso, laughter, tears, and family pictures. We enjoyed seeing mothers of all ages being honored by their children, and somehow, we were connected to a universal Mother.

Mother's Day eventually ended. Alexandra had to take the shuttle back to Washington. Life goes on. To commemorate the day, there's film to develop, picture frames to paint, gifts to share.

The album of continuity is bursting with life. As we pass the torch, we live out this mystery of love and families, and the gift to the world that is motherhood. Every day is Mother's Day to us—we who have the privilege of raising future generations.

Life is no brief candle to me. It is a sort of splendid torch which I have got hold of for the moment, and I want to make it burn as brightly as possible before handing it on to future generations.

— George Bernard Shaw

A Letter to My Readers

Dear Readers,

When I sat down to write a book to celebrate mothers, I was enthusiastic but naive about such an emotional subject. *Mothers*. Just say the word. But what is a mother? Who are these females?

In the process of this personal journey, I've relived my own childhood, I've brought to life my daughters' growing up, and I'm experiencing an expansive sense of rejuvenescence. I feel more alive and abundant today than ever.

I've deepened my respect for mothers and their commitment. I've become more empathetic and compassionate, understanding their fortitude, courage, and ability to support, love, care for, guide, share, and give of their whole self to us, unconditionally, all the time.

Mothers protect the pure, clean, vulnerable essence of others. They allow growth to a deeper self; a natural life energy flows from their authentic, true nature.

The word *mother* conjures up more than a person. A mother is a life force, a spirit. She is living, loving energy, channeling abundance into all of our lives. Being a mother is about having children, but her influence extends far beyond her own off-spring. She is a universal person. Her strength comes gently. What makes her strong is her inherent maternal instincts. A mother is the greatest force in the world.

All females are part of this universal generous energy. Collectively, women nourish, guide, and provide continuity.

Mothers mother. That's what we do. That's who we are.

Bless you,

Alexandra Stoddard

Alexandra Stoddard

Acknowledgments
with Appreciation

To Carl Brandt, Toni Sciarra, Ellen Edwards,
Marysarah Quinn, Elisabeth Carey Miller,
Julie Glen, and Julia Estabrook Hoyt

As my friends you know how much this book stretched me. The process is the most emotionally charged and, because of my struggles, the most thrilling. Thank you for the gift of my writing *Mothers*. This book is truly a celebration. Through your individual contributions, you each played an essential role in the creation of *Mothers*. Thank you for standing by me during this life-changing process.

And to all mothers everywhere, to all women who have acted as mother figures in our lives, I lift you up in great celebration. In the process of writing this book, I relived my own childhood, I relived Alexandra and Brooke's growing up years, and I created a vision of a third childhood. I got in touch with what it's really like to be a woman and a mother. Together, we matriarchs, we *women*, will continue to raise future generations, forever.

Alexandra Stoddard

MAKING CHOICES
71625-9/ $12.50 US/ $15.00 Can

GRACE NOTES
72197-X/ $9.00 US/ $13.00 Can

LIVING A BEAUTIFUL LIFE
70511-7/ $12.50 US/ $15.00 Can

LIVING BEAUTIFULLY TOGETHER
70908-2/ $14.00 US/ $19.00 Can

GIFT OF A LETTER
71464-7/ $10.00 US/ $13.00 Can

DARING TO BE YOURSELF
71578-3/ $14.00 US/ $19.00 Can

CREATING A BEAUTIFUL HOME
71624-0/ $14.00 US/ $19.00 Can

TEA CELEBRATIONS
72324-7/$9.00 US/ $12.00 Can